THE RETURN TO LOVE

Mario Noviello

Copyright © 2017 Mario Noviello

The right of Mario Noviello to be identified as the Author of this work has been asserted in accordance with the Copyright, Designs and Patents Act 1988

All rights reserved. No part of this book may be reproduced, stored in a retrieval system, or transmitted in any form, or by any means, electronic, mechanical copying, recording or otherwise without prior permission from the Publishers.

* * * * *

Published by: *Mario Noviello*

ISBN: 9781521345399

First published 2017

Although every precaution has been taken in the preparation of this book, the publisher and author assume no responsibility for errors or omissions. Neither is any liability assumed for damages resulting from the use of information contained herein.

ACKNOWLEDGEMENTS

First, last, and always, I want to thank the source of Love that gave me the strength, the vision and the passion to write this book. As I wrote the words through the ghost writer that is my soul, I have learned so much about myself and this thing we call life.
I also thank many others: My parents and Grandparents who have shown me nothing but true, unconditional love, my siblings who have always supported and believed in me, my beautiful neice and amazing brother-in-law, and my partner, who's encouragement has been always there for me while discovering this amazing journey of the return to Love.
Finally I would like to thank my editorial team without who's help I could never have produced a book like this.

Cover and book design by *Designed4Print*
www.designed4printdirect.com

Edited by *Verbum Publications*
www.verbumpublications.com

CONTENTS

PREFACE		5
Chapter 1:	**A Return To Love**	17
Chapter 2:	**What is Love?**	33
Chapter 3:	**A Return to Love in Action**	43
Chapter 4:	**A Return to Love in the Present Moment**	70
Chapter 5:	**A Return to Love in Relationships**	78
Chapter 6:	**A Return to Love in Health**	95
Chapter 7:	**A Return to Love in Work and Money**	103
Chapter 8:	**A Return to Love in Acceptance**	118
Chapter 9:	**Finding Peace in A Return to Love**	123
Chapter 10:	**A Return to Love in Happiness**	137
Chapter 11:	**A Return to Love in Death**	152
Chapter 12:	**A Return to Love: The Beginning of an End**	159

PREFACE

I have always had a burning desire to understand how the universe works, what life is really all about, and to seek meaning and purpose for my existence. In reflection, I can see my life has always been something of a devotion – a search for truth and meaning. I was brought up as a Catholic, so having some understanding of the meaning of faith and devotion has certainly shown me a path to take. I have respect for all religions that have a faith and purpose with the intention of bringing us closer to understanding humanity. Often, I feel a sense of guilt for merely being alive – as if I believe God is going to punish me for just being me. Surely a miss-interpretation? But this was bound to occur ... for my philosophy is that all religions are a sign post to the truth but are not the ultimate truth. Believing in God as the creator is only part of it. Only when we personally experience the divine within us can we proclaim it to be the purest truth. My Father was a devout Catholic and my Mother still is, but they never forced upon us a sense of having to believe. They gave myself and my three siblings the space to find meaning and faith by discovering it for ourselves. This liberal and loving upbringing encouraged me to keep searching... and search I did.

I grew up thinking I was subjected to fate. This may be partly true, we don't choose to be born and have no clue as to when we will die. As you will see throughout this book, although fate will always play a part, we can influence our life, shaping it to follow a certain path, but ultimately, life will have the final say. I believe always for the greater good.

I had always oscillated between feeling confident of having control over my life and becoming a pessimistic cynic, believing that the world around me was always against me and I was powerless to do anything about it. Life became a game of love and hate – not hating others, but disliking myself. It can appear quite puzzling and confusing, but one thing we can be sure of is that it is a journey from the cradle to the grave with many unanswered questions along the way.

Some of us live our lives in denial, never confronting the many pains, fears and frustrations we feel, while others will go through life pretending they have all the answers. The injustice, oppression, and cruel realities of the world can easily detract us from our true mission and purpose – living our lives as fully in every respect as we possibly can. Whatever stage of life you are at the question that needs to be asked is who really am I?

As we pass through this brief time we have on earth there are many things that will confuse us and disturb our mental balance. As we seek to find the meaning of happiness, purpose and fulfilment in the midst of a world that is quite broken, we can lose identity of our true self. All we are looking for really is a sense of belonging, understanding how we fit in, and finding a peace within ourselves. This sense of belonging is the true meaning of love; it is intertwined with life itself as where you find love you find life. So, we can say love gives your life meaning and without it there isn't much life at all. This is the essence of what this book is truly about; first remembering, and then redefining your true self, and thus, lovingly awakening the beautiful truth that lies within you. Love has the greatest power capable of changing anything in all of our lives.

I now spend my time teaching and showing others how to find their true purpose and meaning of life. I didn't consciously set out to write this book, it just happened! I had my doubts and fears but I had this kind of force inside of me, always nagging, always there, and it kept pushing me to do it... so I did. I used the techniques described in chapter three to help me. One thing I can be certain about is that it is not our will power that helps us climb mountains but the power of love that prevails to see us through. We are all broken in some way but that shouldn't stop us growing, moving forward, and fully experiencing the enrichment of the life we have. First we must understand our makeup... who we are, our purpose, our mission, then with that wisdom we can move forward. In essence, the difference between someone having and not having something in life is often by choice and not by fate.

To live this life of ours fully we are going to have to love like we have never loved before. Loving cannot be passive, it is direct action you must intentionally take and fearlessly devour to improve your life.

Love is a very powerful thing and those that wield it hold a great advantage over those that don't. It holds no visible authority, it is not a power akin to that owned by a King, Queen or head of state; it contains a different sort of power – one that anyone can have. Not only that, but we finally realise that we are that power. When we are in a state that has us bursting with love, good things are bound to come our way, that's just how amazing love is.

You are your own experience, and what you truly become is yourself.

Life is about us... I, me, myself...everything you experience begins with you and ends with you. This might sound self-centred but ultimately self-expression leads to self-confidence, self-love, self-worth, self-sabotage, self-help and self-control. These all become embodied within us forming one's self-identity. There's a reason why all these start with self... because you cannot find them in anyone else, it all has to come from you. Life begins with one's self and ends with whatever you place in front of yourself, it becomes purely yours to define.

For us to know and remember who we truly are we must look deep within ourselves to understand the principles of the universal laws that govern self-creation. These universal laws not only create our realities but are truly part of us. In fact, the law of creation is literally in our own hands. We are part of the creation process, we are part of a larger whole, and with it we co-create our own life experience.

Before we go any further you must become aware that you are so much more than just your personality, humans have been driven towards a process of over-thinking which is the art of creating problems that weren't even there! People lose their true sense of self because they believe that their opinions, ideas and views form who they are. We tend to stop at any conceptual thoughts about who we really are and then fight them off through self-condemnation not realising that we are the ones who make life happen. We create a reality we don't like, then fight that reality through self-judgment. It is crazy I know, but that is how lost we humans have become. Whatever your opinions are that's all they are, opinions, but as you will see, whatever we attach to and believe to be true we can create through the law of attraction. If you think it is likely to be a bad day, then it will become one for you.

To know the truth is simple; if you feel good from inside yourself then it is the truth you follow. If you feel bad then it's not.

As *Carl Jung* said:

'Until you make the unconscious conscious it will direct your life and you will call it fate. Until we make the truth be known to ourselves we will continue feeling bad about ourselves.'

The more we love the closer we get to God/The Universe/The Primary source ... whatever it is that you believe in. You see, it is about you, and you must first love yourself in order to have the faith to find it in the world and in others. Only that what we have we can receive and thus give unto another.

Failure to recognise that love within you means you will always become a seeker of love. Your soul's mission to love is always in conflict with the mind's unwilling desire to fear this very love. You will soon come to realise either you are moving towards love or you are repelling love at every junction, so before you venture further make sure you know your way. Chasing futile dreams for self-fulfilment that don't serve you only prolongs the emptiness and stops your true self from showing through. In reality most of us don't want to be superman or woman, the only truth we are looking for is that feeling of love, joy, peace and belongingness.

Only the strong can love and only the weak can hate

If you were to ask any person what would be their true wish, the majority would say; a sense of fulfilment, a feeling of belonging, a sense of peace. I am genuinely sad for those who find comfort in the thought of a greater power outside themselves, but I see they are terrified of the power they have inside themselves. Humans are running from themselves it's as if the light, (love), is too good to be true. Their own power overwhelms them. If you have been in the dark for a while, then it can be painful to be awoken by the the light (love again). It takes a tremendous capacity of effort and strength to pierce through this. It takes practice, patience and persistence but it is worth it. Because you are Worth it.

Think of it like this: the universe exists to fulfil itself through you. You are so important but you don't realise that potential within you to be the greatest being on earth. The odds of you being born at the moment you were, are one in four hundred trillion... that's how special you are. You are unique and incomparable.

We all indivisibly and collectively have a divine purpose to be here. What is that purpose and mission? To remember the miracle of love within us. Again the purpose/mission of humans should not be just to remain as human beings but to become beings of humanity. Through growing in awareness we come to realise we are all interdependent ... and through our responsibility of caring for one another we bring our purpose and value to the world. Ultimately we are all one.

Humans have taken different forms to experience the infinite potential life offers to fulfil the divine plan – to experience sublime love and expand love in all creation, multiplying it a thousand fold into the world. Love is the outcome of a profound experience we hold within us that brings us together. We have a huge responsibility to care for one another and for that to take place we must remember the truth of who we truly are. The world promotes self-obsession not self-love. Self-love always joins us together, unlike self-obsession that has the opposite effect of ripping us apart, when we love ourselves we love one and all, by focusing on yourself everything else will eventually fall into place. The endeavour of any human is to feel love, to be appreciated and accepted for who they are, but in the final analysis this process of love-making always starts and ends with you.

Your feelings and emotions are your own, no one else can experience them or have control over them. Whatever you think about in your life – whether you know it to be the case or not, you make a judgment, and a judgment of the imperfections around us will create a boomerang of self-judgment. So, it can be said that an act of kindness towards another is an act of kindness towards ourselves. We are interdependent beings, not totally independent beings. For me to experience love at my deepest core, I need you as my reflection not as my comparison. True love promotes unity not division.

The world today promotes division, independence and for an individual to be encouraged to make it on their own.

'A hundred years ago there was no I, just WE'

Ruby Wax.

We need each other – it is the most beautiful thing to experience when we realise we are whole as one. True love replaces the neediness of our insecurities with the self-fulfilment of love itself. The love you have felt when helping or giving to a friend in need, the help and kindness you show a complete stranger is the best feeling of love you can experience. Humanity needs to remember to love for the sake of it and not for what they make from It.

Love has a mission: for us to know it through first giving of itself.

Life can be said to consist of two dimensions, one is the unseen; your soul, your spirit, your life force, that creates every single situation and experience that appears in your life, the second is the seen; the world you see around you and all the identifications of what it means to you; your careers, your lovers, your status and so on.

The error in thinking comes when you lose your real self in the unreal identification of your mind's attachments to the illusionary world. You see you are the process not the event, these are created by the process of thoughts, words and the actions you take in your life to make them happen. Events and situations have no real power over you, unless you give your power to them. Believing in what is happening outside of your control is undermining your power and diminishing your control. Throughout this book the core message will be to reclaim your power back from your own negative mind-set and from a world that is constantly trying to make you something else.

> *'To be yourself in the world that is constantly trying to make you something else is the greatest accomplishment.'*

Ralph Waldo Emerson

> *'Selfish persons are incapable of loving others but they are not capable of loving themselves either'*

Erich Fromm

The law of attraction is not personal: it delivers exactly back to you whatever you give out in life or believe to be true. It is the physics and mathematics of the universe.

If you suffer it is because of you, if you feel blissful it is because of you. Nobody else is responsible, only you and you alone.

> *'You are the hell and your heaven too.'*

Osho

The secret to healing a belief that you are not an incredible amazing human being, is to love. Love closes the gap between the false and your true self, thus allowing you to become whole again. You don't just have a life, you are life – humans are yearning for the very thing that they are. You will understand that what you were seeking was always seeking you. You can never live a full life if you are always looking for what is missing.

YOU were seeking YOURSELF

You must awaken to who and what you really are. Loving acceptance of ourselves is the catalyst. Love should be seen as a verb – without action it is a meaningless word. The action giving self-love and respect connects with a sense of self-worth in that sacred space inside of you. When you are living in the presence of love then you are revealing your true self. It begins and ends with you, it's nothing to do with anyone else, the circumstances in your life are there to guide you in the right direction back to reality and truth. However, inevitably, negative situations will bring out the poor in us. Anger, stress and anxiousness don't signify the absolute truth, they are merely an emotion we are going through at the time. These negativities need not be defining, but healing. If a repeat occurrence of any given situation comes up in your life it is because it is always something you need to learn from – so let go, or change.

My philosophy is simple: life mirrors back to us what we need to learn from. Heal and love.

A sense of self-worth and respect is not what we receive, but what we give to ourselves and others. The moment you realise this truth is the moment your life will improve.

When you love who you are, what you do will represent that love in every area of your life?

So, what determines your development of a contented life? The self-awareness you hold for yourself. You don't have to create more love in life, for you are love, you just merely need to accept yourself as the miracle that you are. You may not know where your journey will take you but if you include love and grace you are heading in the right direction.

Once you become self-aware of the love you hold within, you will never lose it because that love is your love, the child you were had the secret to life it loved unconditionally accepted, restlessly and fearless you were born to be you, and that will never change. Through great curiosity and a willingness to love like a child, you will find yourself again.

A letter of love: I wrote a letter of love to myself. I would recommend you write a letter of love to yourself. You will need to be honest, transparent and authentic. I can't do this for you, nobody can. Be brave, be yourself. I dare you to forgive not only others, but importantly, yourself.

I promise you will be astounded at how quickly your life turns around. Instead of life feeling like a punishment it will feel an honour to be alive. That is how it is supposed to be – a feeling of peace and joy. Your mission is to become the best self-expression of love on earth that you can be. You are not going to hit the mark every time so there will be times when you will need to forgive yourself. Do it with patience, kindness, compassion, love, and last but not least, self-acceptance.

Many times you will find you need to forgive yourself for not understanding, This will continue to happen until your relationship with yourself is no longer problematic but systematic and in harmony with love itself.

I love you, yes I love you — the being who is reading this book. How do I know that? Why do I say I know you? Because you and I are one. We don't need to have met for love to be felt. In the eyes of love you are me and I am you. We are millions of souls all in one body and we have one purpose – to return to love . . . together.

* * * * *

CHAPTER 1: A RETURN TO LOVE

A return to love is not a place or a far-off destination, it is where we should always aim to be moment by moment as we go through the process of living our life. Most people live in an imaginary place – a dreamland.

Love has been desired from the very beginning of civilisation, and the reason that we can never find it is because love is hidden within us. The paradox that occurs in life is how we desire to live but we cannot live the life we have. Instead, life is the reality of the moment by moment process of living. Generally, most people live in limbo in this imaginary place of loss. The forgotten self is a condition between the two extremes of constantly wanting something from the past, and the future fear of desire. This causes humans to become out of sync with reality and with their true self.

We can never find self-fulfilment in life because it is within us at all times, present between past and future illusions. The reason we cannot find its destination is because it does not exist. Only the journey of living life to the full holds any truth of what love stands for.

This great mystery of love is misunderstood. We question that if love is within us at this very moment, then how can we not feel, experience, or see it in our lives and in the lives of others? How can we believe in love when the world appears so loveless? The monstrosities that are happening in the world can only reinforce the idea that there is no love, and by further extension, no God. I've mentioned God in this section as he is the embodiment of love.

We are here to create God's plan for love, which is for individuals to experience the universe. This universe needed God's plan of love to recognise the experience and for one to know oneself. If love was going to experience itself, it had to have a channel to achieve its goal and self-reflect. So, the world became the great vessel from which love could mirror itself back to us. In doing so, we feel its own essence, sacredness, and beauty.

In the garden of Eden, Adam and Eve were perfected in grace. They had everything; a beautiful home, glorious food, companionship, and beautiful surroundings. So the question is, what went wrong?

Like you and I, they were given free will to think for themselves and be the creator like their father – God, of their own lives. Why was the decision made to eat the forbidden fruit? Was it a metaphor of temptation to make oneself look beyond the immediate perception, which as a consequence caused them to be suddenly cast out of the Garden?

Why would they decide to turn their back on God's word by submitting themselves to the temptation of the snake and possess a desire for greater knowledge?

It was one simple decision; however, they had no ability to experience or show love because they had no knowledge or desire for themselves. The precise moment when they made their decision identified their fall from grace; from this they created a new sense of identity, better known as the ego.

The Freudian concept of the 'ego' is part of the mind that creates a person's self. This creates a sense of an illusionary self to occur between the consciousness and the unconsciousness. We can see the relevance of this within our own lives when we judge ourselves; we literally create a false sense of self which causes us to move further away from our true self. The ego is partly a conscious-thinking subject which creates a sense of personal identity which you yourself consider. It separates itself from the outside world and considers you a separate entity from the rest of nature. We can see the ego is an identity that is false because we both consciously and unconsciously created it. If we take all our beliefs of personality, talents, and abilities, we have the structure of our ego. This fabricated false sense of self is the main reason we suffer from self-delusion, because to base your identity on something that is a concept you created is a fragile and fearful way to live. This is because living your life in a response to mere conceptual thoughts about yourself, obscures you from your real self and from humanity.

Adam and Eve had to create a false identity for they had denied their true selves by looking outside of themselves. Social and cultural behaviours derive from this illusionary mind-set. Taught behaviours from our past have shaped the path of antisocial behaviours based on role plays of our mistaken identity.

Thinking they were anything but whole, caused fear to

automatically rise within both Adam and Eve . It was followed by a bad feeling of shame and guilt. In looking for themselves they had become lost, causing the origin of the sin self-judgment. We can see in our own lives how these truths hold a prevalence; as soon as we judge we begin to feel bad.

Why did Adam and Eve look outside of themselves? It was because they didn't feel good enough. The disassociation of *self* by judging themselves to be not good enough caused a belief system of fear and guilt. We would never feel guilty if we felt good about ourselves and others. The inheritance of this belief system that we are mere fragments of our former selves before the dissociation, that is, before we thought we were anything but whole sacred human beings, couldn't be any further from the truth.

From the very beginning the purpose of humanity was to experience love by creating self-realisation of the soul within the human body. For that to occur, humans needed the opposing limitations and boundaries to enable themselves to evolve. Nothing has ever been achieved without love counteracting fear; to go beyond one's fear is the greatest achievement one can ever experience. In order to achieve, you will need to face the tunnel of fear and see the glimmer of light at the end. Only then will you identify the true, real concept of love. The notion that life is going to be free of fears and insecurities is unrealistic and represents an immature attitude that will bond you with a mind-set of delusiveness. The only place we will ever become free of fear is in the cemetery.

The body represents a limitation of human existence; we are of limited form. Over time, we will get old and die, but within this limitation we have the capacity to experience a life worth remembering. Life is really about the equilibrium in our psychological mind-set, which is the ego. A way to balance this is by loving more and judging less, thus being in control of our negative mind, instead of the ego controlling us.

The mind is a beautiful tool that aids all of creation. It gives us the capacity to receive and store information, but it is not the source of intelligence. Divine intelligence comes from our life force. Our life force is the soul – the true being of self.

The ego is responsible for the misidentification of your true self. You have been separated into two parts: the false sense of self *(ego)* which is unawareness where negative thinking fills the mind of fears, sadness, insecurities and anger, and your true sense of self within your soul where peace, joy, love, completeness, and fulfilment can be found.

While it may be simple to practice appreciating yourself, it is not necessarily easy to be self-aware of the divine love you hold. Love requires effort and discipline for the simple reason that the force that works against your own true self is namely your habitual unawareness and involuntary negative thinking. The mind is automatically and exceedingly tenacious. We tend to be unaware that we are thinking negatively whilst the constant stream of thoughts flow through our minds all the time, leaving us very little respite for choosing love over fear. Inner commitment and a certain kind of work are necessary to sustain this process of self-love creation. Our actions are usually driven by feeding the fear of that false sense of self – the ego's insecurities, rather than choosing to be aware of the part of you that is true sacredness itself.

This can be seen in the story of two wolves:

One evening, an old Cherokee told his grandson about the battle that occurs inside one's soul. He said:

"My son, the battle is between two wolves that are within us. One is evil. It is anger, envy, jealousy, sorrow, guilt, resentment, inferiority, untruthfulness, falsehood, and pride. The other is good: It is joy, peace, love, hope, serenity, humility, kindness, empathy, generosity, truth, compassion, and faith."

The grandson thought about it for a moment, and then asked his grandfather

"Which wolf wins?"

The old Cherokee simply replied,

"The one you feed."

The first step towards freedom involves separating this false-self from the true-self.

Our fore-fathers created doctrines through myths, beliefs, and religions which were introduced to aid us in the journey towards love. But instead of awakening us from our unconsciousness, we fell even deeper into a conscious state of mind creating exterior barriers which we could not penetrate in order to acquire the positive conditions our souls craved.

There have been many masters who walked the planet leaving messages along the way that all relate to the concept of love. Many of these were not Christians, Muslims, or pertained to any particular religious belief, but they were all teachers of love. Like any information passed down from generation to generation their teachings became misunderstood, misinterpreted, and misconstrued. Due to the insecurities of mankind there was created the concept of the blind leading the blind. Jesus once described how these ignorant singers actually caused the power and greed which lead to wars, famine, abuse, and of course, poverty. The question we must ask ourselves on this journey in a return to love, is how much pain do you need to experience before you choose to return? How many delusions do you need to experience before you choose the right action? You are more likely to awaken out of a nightmare than a beautiful dream, but having said this, it is important to consider how sometimes suffering awakens us to the truth that we are sacred beings. This is not the only or the healthiest way to evolve.

The laws God created are in parallel with what applies to the whole of creation; we create our world. This law of attraction isn't personal, or preferable, it is neither physical or visual. The only reason we know it exists is because we exist. Your life force *is* the law of attraction; the law of *creation.*

You can learn to influence your life force by becoming aware of your surroundings which will effectively dictate what your life will become. You are always creating beliefs even though you may not be aware of it. Life is always turned on; it is alive and kicking and forever creating through you. To say you are the universe and the universe is you is closer to the truth of who and what you truly are.

It is mind-blowing to think that we are the co-creators of all creation on a parallel universe, but you will realise the truth when it enters every situation, circumstance, and event. Every positive and negative thought, every bit of our existence, was all first created within our consciousness. In reality, when stripped down to its lowest form, it is no more than our words, thoughts and actions. These words, thoughts and actions carry electro-magnetic vibrational charges that congeal with the same magnetic electrical charges that created matter. These laws date from the very beginning of time: The Big Bang. This was no more than an explosion of love forming universe upon universe of which you are a part of.

As I've said, these laws have been misconstrued due to a misunderstanding by the hierarchies of this world who have purposely hidden this sacred information. If the people of the nations knew who they truly were, the new age of commercialism would have collapsed and the world would not be as we know it today.

The truth shall find its way to every being on this planet, so that every individual shall claim their infinite power back at the right time and place, and in the correct sequence. You will see on an unprecedented level people finding the truth. The second coming is alight within every individual awakening to their true potential and purpose. True love can never be taught or defined; the more important notion is to grow in whom we are, rather than fully comprehend the nature of true love.

Love is a profound experience found deep within us creating the feelings of belonging and wholeness. It is unconditional and cannot be defined, only experienced. The law of attraction, in my theory is also the law of creation; the law of love. It has one agenda which is for us to remember who we are, thus enabling ourselves to experience its wondrous beauty. When you are able to understand that love is purely unconditional, you will see that it will become your purpose to create love with no expectations or rewards. The return of love will be its own reward. When you are able to achieve this then you can say you have mastered the secret and purpose of being human.

So how does this law of love work?

I used to ask Jesus and all the saints I could think of for all things and situations I wanted to happen in my life. Some would materialise and some would not. The things that materialised made me happy in the short term, but after a while the things that didn't appear made me feel more disillusioned. I began to think that the heavens were against me. I felt let down, and my life became increasingly frustrating whilst I carried on, knowing about this law of creation but it was getting me nowhere. Time went by, and the pain I experienced on a day-to-day basis intensified.

I remembered saying to myself, *'I can't stand living like this, I've got to do something'.* As soon as I'd said those words, a sense of peace overcame me. It was a peace which I had never experienced before, and for the first time I accepted that it was I that needed to change and not the world around me. This peace felt different as I now had a voice to accompany it. It told me I had got to grow; it appeared that the answer was given before the question was asked. The acceptance that your life needs to change is the diving board from which to launch yourself into the ocean of life itself. The moment that you make that decision to change, your life changes.

When you are ready to make positive alterations to your life, the changes will always have a positive effect. Life will assist you in every way by attracting whatever you need to help you grow. The irony is that once you have accepted such things needed to change, life becomes easier to manage. You do not need the courage to change, only the will. Months went by and I still had no idea how I was going to change my life. I held in memory, but not in faith, what the soft voice of wisdom had told me. I started to doubt myself as I had done previously in my life. I decided to ask myself again, but this time it was a conscious decision and *not* a question. *I've got to change:* Seconds later the little whisper appeared again, but now with a different message: *If you don't evolve, you'll dissolve.* I understood this loud and clear. I felt excited, and for the very first time I felt comfortable in not knowing. I now understood this to be the miracle of love, holding me in grace. Love can never be seen but it can always be felt within the heart of the person who is ready to receive its wisdom, guidance, and beauty.

As I went in to my local charity shop, a book fell off the shelf. It was *A Conversation with God* by Neale Donald Walsh (a great read which I recommend). In this sacred book, I found the missing piece to my once puzzled life, it was simply: *We are the co-creators of our lives.* I was astounded and emotionally taken aback. I thought life was punishing me by not responding to me. I was waiting for God/The universe, to give me the life I wanted; I had not realised until that point that I had already been given everything I needed. This was the idea that life creates a sacred self that is the being of creation itself. I didn't realise the law of karma was put in place for our growth and not for our penance. *Rhonda Byrne* summarises in her book *The Secret*, that life is responding to you, not happening to you. Life responds to your thoughts and actions.

I realised we could influence our reality by reacting to what we have unconsciously created. This is the fate of the common man who has not found his truth, and relies on fate or destiny to be his reason of sorrow and misfortune.

Aside from experiencing the overwhelming feeling of relief, I also felt a crushing feeling of fear, as that was the moment I realised I was solely responsible for my life and I could no longer play victim to blame and judgement.

So the question becomes, how does the law of love work within you and why? God gave us free will to take the path we choose, to enable us to become the creators on earth. In essence he made us creators to experience the love and infinite possibilities on Earth. We were made self-sufficient to conduct our own lives the way we choose.

It is hard to believe and comprehend but it is true. All we will ever need is already here buried in the sacred files within your consciousness. The railway track was laid before man made the train. This phenomenon we call creation is a backward process. As I write this book the words were present long before I ever existed. My process is to write the words from my starting point. Every song ever performed already existed; it was just waiting for the right channel to be delivered through. Every invention came from somewhere. The manifestation of creation happened. It forms through our thoughts and feelings, and from those two notions, deeds are created. Our world then creates from that certain situations – from everything we say and do. The law of love records and responds with reaction; this is the law of karma. When you realise that you are the designer of your reality you become the incredible deliberate creator.

As *Buddha* said:

'All that we are is the result of what we have thought.'

Humanity lost itself from the very beginning because so much of our thoughts had been directed outside of ourselves, thus missing the true meaning of our journey.

The creation of life always starts with feelings. These feelings are no more than an energy frequency that attracts equivalent emotions. Thoughts congeal themselves in these frequencies to manifest a reflection of ourselves in this world. What appears to be solid and real is no more than fluctuating energy. The truth of how the universe works is simple – love is within you, and you are within the universe, which is within God. This is the one life source.

It is only your reflection that you see in the world, so why have we created a life not fitting for an alien? Why the struggle, the frustration, the illness? Why the heart aches, the fear the pain. Why do we suffer so much? All these question can be answered clearly. We thought we were not good enough; actually, we were taught we were not good enough. This can be traced back from the original sin of judgement of self from the very beginning.

Very few people have found the cure to the feeling of not being good enough. You can be the richest, most famous and powerful man or woman on the planet, but if you have not found the divine and sacred force within you, you will always be accompanied by this curse. In fact, you will feel it even more profoundly, because the world has taught you that to feel complete and good enough you have to have all the treasures, protect them, and guard them with your life. You are the gift to the world. The world means nothing if you don't exist. You give meaning and beauty to life itself.

The human race is facing two problems: The first is that they have forgotten who they are. The second is that they are following someone else who has also forgotten who they are. Both of these are illusionary. You are the co-creator of your destiny. Most people are not aware of the power they hold inside them as they drift through life like sheep being herded along the way. However, the decision to make a change where you turn your back on the values and beliefs of the other people around you is just one step away.

So what are the choices? Either you return to love or you remain in fear. You decide whether you want to prioritise your life or allow someone else to do it for you, and that may not always be the way you want. If you base your life on status, this will rob you of your true peace.

What you call life is actually your unseen self – the soul that gives life to every single creation in your human form. As I write these words I know them to be the truth and it is only when we hear the truth that it will be able to resonate from within you. We can say that this is a self-educating process of the memory.

In order to taste anything such as your favourite fruit for example, you must first eat it; you must feel the sensations on your taste buds. If I was to tell you that a strawberry tasted amazing, you can only believe me, taking my word for it. However, it will stay in the realms of your conceptual thought and so becomes a mere belief of what a strawberry actually tastes like. You have never actually experienced the taste for yourself. This analogy demonstrates that life needs to be acknowledged, practised, then remembered within ourselves and not in a way acquired simply by believing others.

Your life begins with self-love, self-respect, self-kindness, self-dignity, self-compassion, self-worth, and self-esteem. There is a reason why they all begin with self – because your life can never be found in anyone else. You must learn to honour, cherish and love yourself. Your first relationship therefore, *must* be with yourself. Be yourself, and the world will adjust. Don't try and force yourself to fit in when you have been created to stand out.

Now we know how the illusion occurred, why it happened, how life is created, and how the law of love works. The next stage is to carry on with what we came here to do, which is to evolve to the next level in our evolutionary process. This is the very purpose of your being here: Return to love and create love on earth. There is nothing but love flowing through you, if you do nothing with it, the sacred you stays absent.

Now, place your hand on your heart. Feel that? That beating is a miracle. You are alive for a reason. Everything cannot be explained but trust that there is a reason and through love all will be made apparent.

The moment humans were born they began a decent back home but where is that home? Home is where the heart is. Home is where love resides within you. The universe is very patient, but it is also relentlessly seeking to express its love. The universe needs you for its very existence; it needs your cooperation to move to the next level. The divine plan for us is to return to love.

Your soul's mission is to experience its own sublimity and it will never stop searching until the sacred truth is found. When you have really expressed love, you will never forget that love is you.

How do we return to love?

I shall give you 7 tools which will enable you to recognise and return to love in a way that is active and practical to implement. These *Spiritual Practices* have been designed for you to use in a daily routine.

I will reference the appropriate *Spiritual Practices* where they become relevant throughout the book.

In this Chapter: *Spiritual Practice 2* is *First: Love Yourself.*

Action will need to be taken, discipline and intentional focus given. All the asking and praying in the world won't help you until you take action and responsibility for your own life, but remember, love itself is the simplest, and really the only way return to the forgotten self.

CHAPTER 2: WHAT IS LOVE?

Love is state of being, a vibratory energy frequency of infinite motion. It is an invisible force that can never be seen, but always experienced through a human consciousness which is more advanced than that of other primates. Being conscious in this sense is to be self-aware of something within oneself. The only difference between humanity and the animal kingdom is that humans are conscious of being alive; we have been given the grace to know ourselves through self-awareness. True self-awareness is the coming together of body, mind and spirit. This unity of truth allows us to become conscious of the love we hold, and for it to flourish in life there needs to be that element of recognition, focus and attention.

If self-deprivation denies us love, then it will be absent from our experience. All creatures need attention in order to exist and thrive. It can be said that love needs itself to recognise its presence. You are the highest state of being – you are human, and the process of becoming conscious of love is brought about through the focus on *self-love*. The reason why some people experience a greater fulfilment in their lives than others is not because of luck or chance, but because they somehow naturally have an ability to be able to focus attention on their life. They are truly capable of loving themselves and others unconditionally. This creates a more satisfying life pattern and greater for our consciousness of love to grow. The more we grow in our awareness the more we create a welcoming life full of excitement, expansion and joy.

Our creator created us in the image of perfection. This desires only one thing, to express its love through you. This pure adoration has only one goal in all of creation, and that is to give unconditionally with no exception or expectation. To love ourselves in this way causes a truly phenomenal experience to take place within us. This can never be found, touched, or felt, anywhere but inside of ourselves.

Ask yourself: Have you experienced anything outside your existence? It's impossible.

We're all guilty of seeking pleasure by basic instinctive means, but if we look deeper within ourselves we will come to understand that we must recognise this adoration within us by unconditionally loving ourselves first.

Our one true mission is to know ourselves. If you keep denying the treasures of love within yourself, you will rarely experience the goodness of life, for love is life. We cause so many problems for ourselves when we starve our natural feelings, it will affect every level of our existence. In general, the less love we feel, the more we need to feed the body with all kinds of unhealthy things. If we fix the problem of not first loving and caring for ourselves enough, then life becomes easier, and, literally amazing.

We can see when this process is beginning to work. Things start to change for the better. This will ignite the law of cause and effect whereby the effect will be the growth and expansion of affection in your life. That is why it is known as the great multiplier, for whatever we focus it on will expand and grow in beauty.

As your love intensifies you will feel a self-realisation of who you truly are. This transcendental state is where your mind, body and soul amalgamates. It can be compared to the Holy Trinity – a coming together of all parts of the whole being. When this is done a feeling of integrity returns to one's life again. You will find the more you love yourself the more you will see yourself as part of everything and separate of nothing. Only when you look at the world this way will you be capable of really loving.

We have a responsibility to take care of one another but before we do we must gain the first-hand experience necessary. Love has certain qualities: compassion, humility and kindness. These three qualities encompass all the other values it stands for; in compassion, you will find strength, honesty, loyalty, integrity and understanding; in humility, you will find wisdom, unity, acceptance, authenticity, meekness and gentleness; and in kindness you will find the most important quality that embraces all the others – sharing.

To be kind is to be generous of self, which is love's true nature and purpose. Acts of kindness makes us feel good, alive and valuable; this is your soul's purpose of being. Acts of kindness will unite all the qualities in one single process, making a difference that has a lasting, rippling effect, which undoubtedly will change not only your life but the lives you touch. When performing an act of kindness your soul joins with another – there is a *oneness.*

Subtle changes start to take place when you can harness love within yourself. An authentic optimism and a feeling of just being so alive will return to your life. This can be likened to our life as a child which seemed so uncomplicated and beautiful.

So how can we finalise the true identity of love? By knowing that it is you. It is the core of your very being. The moment a soul is reincarnated it remembers itself, but without your cooperation it can't be expressed until you build that relationship and return to love. There is a part of you – your higher self, that remembers your perfection – the true essence of purity that lies within you. Your purpose of living right now is to first reconnect with this feeling and then push it out into the world again so that others too will recognise it and so the perpetual chain of its divine actions can begin.

Love is divine wisdom and grace. A new born child is perhaps its purest form, but it can never remember. A baby instinctively knows who it is. This state of purity is only temporary as the baby has to evolve in order to flourish as a human being.

Life cannot be hidden, it must not be inactive, because a suppressed life is a depressed soul. Evidence of this suppression is all around us and the time we are living through now is unprecedented in human history. Never have we seen our planet in such disarray, such agony and confusion. Change is part of the evolutionary process; we are here to grow, but our own lower self is hindering our progression as human beings and is stopping us from experiencing the true honour of the life we hold within us. You have a duty. *Albert Camus* once made this clear by stating:

'I know of only one duty, and that is to love'.

Passivity and activity are polar opposites. As a human being you have to take action in the return to love. An intentional daily action towards this will anchor you to the truth. Nothing can be achieved without the passion that only the love in you can ignite. Your dreams of better relationships, good health, and infinite abundance all start with you. Knowing its qualities will naturally gravitate you towards applying love to every situation; the steps you then take will always include self-respect, courage, clarity and integrity.

Love is the binding agent that brings humanity together. Your ability to generate the powerful feelings from its power is unlimited. When you do this you are in complete harmony with the universe. It will always lead you down the path of integrity, honesty, kindness, humility, compassion, and gratefulness. It is the most powerful force in the universe and you are that force. To allow this to grow within you to aid your life, you must be only willing.

Until we allow this force to become prominent it will instead remain in the background of our lives ... waiting. If we search for it outside of ourselves in factors we cannot control it will only lead us to a *forgotten self*. When you project your lack of adoration onto the world, you accuse the world of not loving you enough, and all you are able to perceive is an unfriendly world. Love does not judge you; you do that to yourself. It never abandons you, despite the fact we often abandon ourselves. You need to be willing to accept yourself and love yourself daily, no matter what.

You are not at the receiving end of the universe; all that you are seeing in the world is your state of being. Your worth is not in the hands of others but in your own. When we accept ourselves, we allow others to accept themselves also. God didn't create imperfection, we labelled perfection imperfect; the universe doesn't make mistakes – you are perfect. Know your infinite worth – you are a God with a body.

Until you practice harnesing the most powerful emotional experience humans can have in this way, you won't know what you are capable of. It is the miracle that grows; the inner strength and confidence self-love gives you is a pass to move beyond the past, beyond fears, and beyond ego – the false veil that blurs the boundaries of lies and truths to satisfy our mind. From pain to joy, from the small insignificant feelings of yourself to the vastness that you truly are, love is the gateway through which, once entered, you will meet your true self again.

Our sole purpose on this planet is to learn about unconditional love. This begins by witnessing it for ourselves through pure self-adoration. This is not a vanity; that comes about by making the assumption that your life exists outside of you and all you can ever be is an idea of yourself – not actually yourself. It derives from the fear or not feeling good enough. A grandeur of narcissistic righteousness hides the persona of someone who feels very small. Adoration goes beyond the dualities of being right or wrong by wanting to be seen in a certain way. It is the centre of everything; compassion, caring, and understanding. If we don't allow ourselves to love who we are then we can't give it out to others. We cannot give what we do not have. As I began to love myself, my relationship with everyone changed: I saw the world through different eyes, I experienced more, kindness, joy, and peace with others, the less I projected my fear, pain, and unhappiness onto the world the less I experienced back. As we stop judging ourselves we judge others less. The more I loved, the less defensive I became. The joyousness felt within becomes the greatest gift you can have, because as you then give it of yourself, others experience the feeling of affection through your actions.

To have a constant sense of self-worth and self-value is the most amazing feeling, but how do we love ourselves? Self-love cannot be just a thought or merely a way of thinking. Real fondness that lasts is a presence before we give it a name. Expressing that we love ourselves through thoughts, words, and images, triggers our attention towards what is already within us and around us. Love is all about allowing this to happen. As we shift our attention our experiences change. If we seem to become emotional by listening to a song on the radio whereas a minute earlier we were perfectly happy, all that happened was a shift in our focus to cause that experience. This wonderful emotion is already within us; it appears as our experience when we *allow* it to be just that.

Giving it your full attention, ask love to support you with forgiving yourself and others. Ask it to remind you to be more patient and grateful for what you already have, and to guide you on life's journey. Don't always beseech material things; man cannot live on bread alone. The love within you has every answer to every question. Ask this higher intelligence, it is quintessentially who you are. Ask, and you shall find yourself in the right place at the right time and know all you need to know.

As we intentionally apply all of this, past emotions, fears and doubts will come to the surface, and emotions we didn't even know existed will be remembered. This process of inner cleansing is perfectly natural. Whenever we love we literally raise our vibratory energy frequency – the life force within us. Whenever we do this everything else rises too, so, as these emotions come forward say yes to them. Give them your full attention, then carry on loving yourself even though you may have doubts. Knowing that you are an amazing incredible beautiful human being starts with a conscious decision to turn away what feels bad about yourself and move towards what feels good. The person who realises that they, and they alone create their own reality, has the world in their hands. It is like going to the cinema and not liking the movie: you can get up and walk out of the theatre and go and watch another movie. You see, shifting your attention to another thought presents a new kind of show.

Allow your attention to sink deeply into whatever you desire about yourself. Remember that from here on in, we are all experiencing our own movie. Our consciousness is reflecting our current state of being. We are always at the centre of our experience, everything is inside of you, nothing exists outside your hemisphere. Nothing is over there in life we are never separated from whom we are. If we are to experience what we truly desire, we must apply the principle to our present. If you imagine what you decide to be in the future, you will always generate a continuous state of delay. If you are constantly projecting the *'it's not here yet'* attitude, then your vibratory state of being will send out this feeling and you shall receive back the same – resulting in the *'never getting there'* State of mind.

Don't take your circumstances too seriously, it is not these that create your state of being, but rather your state of being creates your circumstances. If we can perceive every situation as optimistic, you will find that your frequency will align itself to whatever experience you wish to gain from that particular circumstance. The next moment of your reality will reflect this and you will attract a positive result in return. The main message is to feel amazing and love where you are right now.

Remember, you are the giver and the receiver of every experience you will ever have. You can never be separated from creation, for you are the one who is creating it. You must not be afraid of this power or else you will fall victim of your own creation. Be your own guardian; when you feel afraid you are actually giving your power away. Pay attention when you feel low or afraid, it is not the real you; this is your unconsciousness – the ego – past historical stories forming a negative picture in your mind. The truth is when we feel bad, it is not our true self. When we feel this affection, let it be a reminder that you can change the way you feel by changing your state of mind. Know you can choose how to feel at any given moment by merely replacing your thought with another thought – by changing your perspectives from a lower-self of unconscious beliefs to higher-self. It feels amazing.

To feel good about ourselves we must feel worthy of doing so. Ask yourself is it ok to just feel good about myself? By asking this you will open the gateway of allowing yourself to feel good about yourself. It is what this world needs. Be the person you would prefer to become; be excited to be you, it is not selfish to love and care for yourself. The more you care about you the more you will care about others. It will be your decision to allow yourself to love yourself and be whatever you want to be. Remember, we are all one being. When you feel loved, make sure to pass this feeling onto others. Know you are a powerful creator, and as we realise this personal power, we become truly humble and grateful.

So how do we return to love and create our own reality?

In the next chapter I shall present you with *7 Spiritual Practices*, which will enable you to recognise and practise returning your mind to this state of love, joy, truth, power, and integrity. It will require discipline, focus, and continuous practice in order to manifest your true identity.

CHAPTER 3: A RETURN TO LOVE IN ACTION

Love is all about action. Love is a verb found in the act of making something happen. There is no cause for waiting for it to suddenly occur, it is a decisive action that needs to be experienced. The law of creation can only be cohesive through our own willingness; you are the final authority, not me, not God, your spouse, or your government. None of these influences can bear responsibility for your life or actions. Of course, you can pretend to give up this ultimate authority, or ignore it and act as though you haven't got it. Ultimate authority is quite amazing, it means you already have the power to take action. You are fully equipped to do so, but you need strategies to help you. For us to experience an amazing life we must take positive daily action in achieving this new reality.

Remembering who we truly are takes practice, patience, and persistence to change the way we think speak and act. It takes action to break through the layers of past mis-information about who we thought we were. So go easy on yourself.

Positive daily action eradicates negative thinking, removing the memories of failures and disappointments, missed opportunities and anxieties over the future. By actively loving yourself you create a space within you where inspiration and intelligence exists. This sentient intelligence is love in action.

A positive attitude hands you power over your situations, rather than your situations having power over you.

The notion that life can give you anything without action is a scam perpetuating from the new mis-informed generation who believe life owes them something. Life doesn't owe you anything; it is all about participation, dedication, and the action of self-expression. Only through action can you see the reflection of true meaning and purpose in the world. If you want to feel loved you've got to be loving, if you want your life to have meaning, you have to give it meaning. Not all actions are positive; you can work very hard and achieve very little. So make sure your intent is driven by passion and not by persuasion of the mind to simply try and become more in the eyes of the world. Actions say a thousand words. Start with what you would love to achieve, life really has no purpose until you can give it one. The universe is waiting for you to make the first move.

You will achieve great things in a relative short space of time as long as your actions are clear and decisive. Life will bring forth opportunities, and when it does, you should be sure not to miss them.

I have 7 strategies you can follow. What you will realise as you read through them is that they are born from inside you. For this reason, I call them *Spiritual Practices*. When you recognise them, you will understand how implementing them will aid your journey back to love and firmly establish your success. Each Spiritual Practice will draw on the law of creation from within you. Honour and abide by them and use them to create the amazing life that you were always meant to experience.

Spiritual Practice 1: *Choice is a simple decision*

You must decide for yourself what road your life will take as it will always lead you somewhere. It is up to you. Your thoughts, words and actions become your decision. There are many realms in your sub-consciousness and it is your relationship with these realities that form your life. Our lives are a reflection of our choices, of who we are and who we choose to be. It is not your parents, your past relationships, your job, the economy, the weather, an argument, or old age that is to blame. You, and only you are responsible for every decision and choice you make. Nothing else is to blame.

You can't escape the principle that for twenty-four-seven you are attracting a creative stream into your life that is forging your experiences. You can't stop this mechanism, you are inseparable from it. Existing beyond time and space, it is permanently and infinitely forever creating. You exist in a timeless state, and for this very reason life never stops its' creation process. Many people overlook this. It is like watching the same movie thousands of times over; if we don't consciously decide to change the channels we will watch re-runs forever more. Ground hog day will become our fate.

Most humans are only concerned with the state they are presently in, not with how they got into that state in the first place. This is where we get stuck in a cycle of experiences of a reality that we unconsciously created. What most people will define is what they judge, and ultimately, base their future decisions upon. We create situations and circumstances that we don't like and then judge them to be bad, but, you see, the reflection you receive is based on what you were unconsciously thinking and feeling.

We have become obsessed with asking ourselves *'what is?'*

When we do this we bring it into our reality. Thinking something is real and believing it can never be changed is the worst mistake: *'What is?'* is a reflection of *'What was.'* You are basing your reality on the past.

You have to *decide* to think and feel different thoughts that will raise your vibratory frequency – the life force energy that determines what you have. If you are only able to see the *What is?* Then, by the law of creation, you will create only *more* of what is. You must be able to put your thoughts beyond that in order to attract something more. If you wish to experience a new reality, you have to persistently, everyday, choose what you would prefer to be. This way of living needs to become your number one passion. If the state of your consciousness is not your number one priority then life will have its way with you. Your unconscious thoughts will create your experiences without your permission. If you do not show a level of commitment to the way you are living from day to day, then you will never be able to take responsibility for the fact that every reflection is your own choice. Remember, whatever we are being we are receiving.

If you cannot admit that every experience you have is a reflection of your choice, then you are not ready for a higher state of spiritual maturity. If we do not consciously decide to care how we think for ourselves every day, then we will become the embodiment of all the negative emotions we have gathered. Through this we end up punishing ourselves and our life becomes a random generator of events.

In truth, we do not want to be responsible for our own state of being because it seems like hard work. This is not the case. It does require a great degree of dedication, commitment, and desire to enable us to recognise our responsibility. By stepping up to the fact that we desire to be a master of our own creation, we begin to accept our own choices and decisions.

Ninety-nine percent of the process of making a decision comes from within us, from the law of creation at work. Only one percent reflects the process of is how it was actually created. Your choice is under your command. The first and most important step to take towards your preferred lifestyle is by having the ability to decide. Life is your state of mind, if we don't know what to choose, our life will represent our confusion.

Everyday ask yourself; *What do I choose to experience today?* Ask this question as soon as you wake up, and every time you have a decision to make. Never miss a day of asking yourself this, as the moment you make that decision – your life changes.

Learn to choose for yourself and do not enter a passive state of being. Decide the state of mind you choose to be, all you need to do is know yourself. Decide who you want to be, and never mind about figuring this out as we are constantly changing. You will come to know yourself as you pass through the various stages of your life, and each time you will experience something different.

The real question is: What do you decide to be and what do you base this decision on? Use your experiences as guidelines to who you truly want to be. Look beyond the physical mind-set. Remember, do not wait for anything. Follow your path and make the choices as life presents itself. We all have the potential, so put it into action by choice. Remember, use this time to think big when it comes to your life.

Decide and choose the outcome of what you want in life. Feel it within your heart. This is the only thing you need to do, the rest will follow in its path. Deciding and determining who you are through choice is the only way to live your life. This first spiritual practice, will truly harness the love back into your life.

When you are ready to make positive changes in your life you will attract whatever means are needed to help you on your journey. Life is actually a choice. Be willing and ready to change. Your first choice is always to love and accept yourself in whatever situation you may find yourself, then decide to choose again until you feel good about yourself.

The moment you make a decision, your life changes.

Learn to choose for yourself don't remain in a passive state of being. Decide on the state of mind you choose to be in. All you need to do is know yourself.

How do you know yourself?

By deciding who you want to be. Trying to figure out who we are is over-rated. If you are in a constant state of trying to figure out who you are, I promise, you will always be confused. This confusion will always lead you to relying on the opinions of others. Start by deciding to love yourself. Experience that love. The miracle occurs as we consciously manifest our own reality. We see what we want to be, we become bold and fearless. What happens through this conscious self-defining process is that you begin to feel yourself as the creator of your own destiny, and what then occurs with some accuracy is that you start to know what does and doesn't resonate for you.

If what you feel and think excites you then it's going to be what your soul wants for you. Remember this: Whatever you want, wants you more. You will experience an abundance of joy in creativity as these are qualities your higher-self desires to be expressed and experienced through you.

Think about this for a second: all you have ever wanted comes not from the world around you but from inside yourself. So, through the process of choosing who you prefer to be, you figure things out much more quickly than if you waited to find out.

Think big: if you're going to think anything you might as well think big.

It may feel you are deluding yourselves at first when choosing consciously what you prefer to be, but what we must remember is that no reality is certain, all can change, because you are the one creating it. Remember first and foremost, everything you think, say, and do, is a reflection of what you've decided about your life. It is the way you decide to think about yourself and others that causes your life to be either amazing or miserable. The power of decision gives you the power to change anything in your life. The law of creation is always working in the background, duplicating what you value most, be mindful in what you choose to think, say, and do.

Decide and choose the outcome of what you want, feel it within your heart in the here and now. Life is going to give you back just what you put into it, so put your whole heart into everything you do.

By the act of choosing you reclaim your power. Choice is the most honourable gift you can give to yourself. Making this decision for yourself is the first spiritual practice that will truly harness love back into your life.

Spiritual Practice 2: *First: Love yourself*

What most people don't realise is that the love they experience is the embodiment of who they are. If you cannot love who you are, then you cannot love anyone else to the fullest. There is a part of you that knows the essence of pure love, this connectivity within yourself was lost the moment you entered the material realm. You inherited the conceptual belief system that you weren't good enough. Due to this humans have been searching for the very thing they are in true essence from the beginning of time. The world has lost its truth, this can be witnessed by the teachings of the world. It is the last place that love can be taught. In fact, it promotes the exact opposite – fear. Fear represents a human soul which is lost in the illusion of a love-less world. The world says to be loved you must reach perfection in character and that it must be earned. It is inconceivable to think that a child of God is not worthy of receiving what is rightfully theirs, so the promotion of love is sold to the person whose goods are already theirs. To love yourself before anyone else is actually a selfless act, not a selfish one. Love comes from the self-awareness of the love within YOU. If you can't love yourself, how can you love anyone else? Therefore, you must first recognise the love within you to experience the love you give. The process of love has always been focused on the beloved not the lover. This error in thinking causes an endless yearning for love's approval and acceptance by others. You have to love yourself so passionately, so intensely, that everything and everyone becomes one in that love. We are all a united being – the whole of humanity. Only when we love ourselves can the true meaning of love be felt between you and the wider world around you. Love first and see what you can do with that love.

Loving yourself is a gift that you can give back to the world. This is your second spiritual practice to act upon.

Spiritual Practice 3: *Never judge yourself.*

Your life is never going to change simply by complaining about yourself. Self-pity is very destructive. For most humans, this unconscious negative behaviour of judging one's self causes life to be something to endure just to get through to survive. A judgmental attitude is a very precarious way to live. To condemn another is to condemn oneself.

'Those who want to destroy the world around them actually want to destroy whatever shame they carry within themselves.'

When you make a judgment of another person you are casting a judgment on yourself. Don't contaminate your sacred space. You can only really be free in life when you stop doing this. Remember, nothing is good or bad unless you start judging it to be so.

We need to know love can never be felt in the past or future. That way of thinking exists only in conceptual thoughts that your mind/the ego has created.

The quickest way back to inner love and peace is to discontinue judgment. Contrary to popular belief everybody has their insecurities ... a story of heartache to tell. It doesn't matter what these are that hold true for you, as long as you release them by acknowledging that you own them.

10 things you own but can give up:

1. Excuses

2. Self-doubt

3. Fear of Failure

4. Procrastination

5. People-pleasing

6. Fear of Success

7. Negative thinking

8. Negative self-talk

9. Judgment of yourself and others

10. Negative people in your circle

Through the commitment of observing you're flaws you have the power to create a new reality of love.

At best you can say we are all perfectly flawed, but that should not stop us growing, moving, and experiencing the life we have.

Nothing holds you back more than your insecurities. Learn to embrace love and accept yourself instead of falling victim to self-judgement.

Spiritual Practice 4: *Self-talk*

Self-talk is the most important strategy of all; by changing the way you think, you will inevitably change the way you feel which will have an effect on all situations in life. Self-talk is a necessity to harness love back into your life. Through it you become your own best friend; someone you can rely on and that will never leave you. You will see yourself as someone that you admire and respect. Think about the words you would you use to describe someone you totally admire and respect and use them for yourself to awaken your true identity.

In order to work within the natural laws of creation intelligently, love must be impregnated and infused within your thoughts, words, and actions. Love is the product of all emotions; it is essential they can be controlled and guided by your intellect and reason. It is love that imports vitality to thoughts and thus allows them to germinate allowing the law of creation to bring the necessary material for growth and maturity and manifestation of what we desire. Therefore, if we wish for desirable conditions we can afford to only obtain desirable thoughts and use desirable words, as words are the representation of our thoughts taking form. We must be especially careful to use only constructive and harmonious language which, when finally crystallised into object form, will prove to our advantage. When we use any form of language which is not identified with love, truth, dignity, and compassion, we take ourselves away from the core truth. Everything we think, say and do must be impregnated with love.

Self-talk changes your thoughts which entails changing your feelings. Your feelings are far superior than the words and thoughts that precede them; they are the energy vibrations behind the thoughts and words spoken. These frequencies are magnetic and are the life force behind your manifestations. Your life unfolds to a pattern exactly as the feelings it is spoken through. The words we speak are very powerful. Our inner dialogue has become very negative and so has our self-talk. This is because every time you deny a feeling of love the highest thought about yourself, you actually fear it. Humans fear their greatness more than their smallness, and by denying your true self you deny a piece of your sacred self too.

If thoughts are creating our reality, why aren't we creating what we wish to create? You are always successful in creating, but it may not be what you want. The only thing that is stopping you is resistance which comes from self-belief. The number one success to failure is he who believes it is not possible. If you believe something is impossible then you are creating that reality, and you will achieve that very thing. The only way to change the lack of belief about yourself is simple – begin thinking opposite to the negative thoughts that already consume your mind. As you consciously think thoughts that move into words of vitality of higher value and self-worth you begin to change the programming in your subconscious mind. It is like a computer storing messages, thoughts and feelings that either yourself or others have believed to be true of you. The subconscious of your being is the core of what we hold at this epic centre of our inner being. Whatever you hold in your subconscious is what happens in your life. It stores thoughts that create feelings that ignite creation. Once the subconscious mind has a new programme it must use it to change reality. This is why self-talk is so important. As you start to consciously think new thoughts and use new words and images that are clearly infused with a higher value and worth, you begin to experience your own truth and beauty. I would like to invite you now to take part in a spiritual practice that will ignite the love within you. This invitation must be accepted if you are to change your life into something amazing. Before we enter the sacred space of love I give you a warning: You will come up with internal resistance, you will sense a feeling of rejection from your own subconscious mind. Don't be alarmed, this is perfectly normal and it is the safety trigger ensuring you are ready for your new reality. Acknowledge these feelings and carry on.

Try this for seven days: Choose a place where you can be alone, preferably in the morning as the mind is clear of all clutter after the process of sleep. Take a deep breath and exhale. This will ground the words within you. Then, say:

'I am willing to love myself'

Say this out aloud. Words have more vibrational energy force behind them when spoken out aloud. They shift from being tools of wishful thinking to tools of action. Remember to exhale and inhale deliberately, but keeping the rhythm natural at all times during this process. Notice that your feelings may offer resistance. Feelings and sensations of agitation, tension – even anger, may arise. A disbelieving mind can be very stubborn. Don't allow this to phase you, be determined, and focus.

Keep breathing in rhythm, then repeat: *'I love you'* and this time add your *name*.

Repeat a third time saying: *'I really love you, you are amazing,'* followed again by your name. Say *'thank you'* to end the sentence. Gratitude is the recognition of anything good. When you intentionally direct love back to yourself you will experience a feeling of goodness returning. You can never recognise love without appreciation. Gratitude anchors that feeling within you.

Repeat the process of self-love through self-talk until you feel the love ignited within. Be the reflection of what you would like to receive. The world doesn't owe you anything, life is all about participation, so invest in yourself. You're worth it.

The next step in a return to love is to take your love with you wherever you go. Consciously bring it out with you: When out walking say *'I love you, you are amazing.'* When washing the dishes say it also. Wherever you are, whatever you are doing, use self-talk at every opportunity. To acquire more love, fill yourself with it, until you become a magnet for love.

We have thousands of thoughts every day. Make them loving thoughts. Loving people live in a loving world and unfriendly people live in an unfriendly world. You are the one who decides which world you want to live in.

Use and make declarations of light energy words which are full of kindness compassion and love. Speak with a conscious tongue. Say only those things you truly wish to experience. Do not speak about negative things that you do not desire, doing so will cause them to come about.

I have made a few suggestions below for alternative light words you could use to ignite the feeling of love and build your self-esteem. However, the essential point is that as we should create a unique life for ourselves we therefore should create our own confirmations for the life we choose to experience. Use whatever words resonate with you to draw and recognise the goodness that lies within you.

1. *I love and accept myself.*

2. I am wonderful and beautiful.

3. There is enough love for everyone, including me.

4. I am loved wherever I go.

5. Life loves me.

6. I am loving and loveable.

7. It is safe for me to love myself here and now.

8. I approve of myself exactly as I am.

9. I am willing to give myself love and receive love.

10. I love my body.

11. I am worth loving

Become aware that the words you habitually choose affect everything about yourself. You are always thinking, so you are always creating and directing your subconscious mind in the direction of your experiences.

As I wrote this book, all I would tell myself was I can do it... and I did. Perhaps now you are beginning to understand that whatever the mind can conceive can be achieved. Infinite realities already exist; the formations of these realities is dependent on letting go of the negative resistance you hold towards believing you can achieve them. By applying self-talk to our daily lives through practice and not just theory, we will achieve our goal. The more you dedicate yourself the more you see you are the miracle that has already happened. Say it, feel it, be it. This process goes far deeper when you *really* believe.

Choose a thought you want to experience, pick a thought right now – any thought. If you are hesitating, you can try these as examples:

I am amazing, I am incredible, I am beautiful.

See that becoming true for you. We are only a thought away from anything. If you are sceptical of this, ask yourself, has your life been anything more than what you have believed it to be? Reflect on these words, you will not be able to deny the fact that you, and you alone have created the life you see before you. There are no secret thoughts. Look at your life and realise it has become a reflection of what you have been thinking. *Think* consciously.

Spiritual Practice 5: *Imagination and Visualisation*

Imagination is one of the greatest instruments you can use to harness love back into your life. Imagination is the most powerful spiritual practice; if you can see it, feel it, and believe it, you can have it. This is the secret to all creation, as imagination is consciousness, and consciousness becomes who we are.

You are not just stuck with one life, you are as many realities as you feel. There are many parallel realities, and when you imagine them you can step into new life-forms time and time again. We can never imagine something which isn't real. It has to exist if we are to imagine it, and if we can imagine it, then it bears some level of truth. We draw to ourselves the replica of that we have imagined.

At the centre of the universe dwells the great spirit of imagination waiting to form within you. Every imagination has a magnetic vibrational frequency that attracts the same reality in shape, colour, and form. A day dream is not always a waste of time, it is actually a place where new reality comes out to play in the mind. It can be a blueprint for your future, and your future can never be more real than now; the now is the starting point of all that will ever be. Imagination is so powerful, you can become whatever you feel this very moment.

Dare to imagine for yourself a completely different reality. Remind yourself that you don't have to do what everyone else is doing. In fact, our most vivid imaginations as children held the secret of our higher-self – our soul's, utmost desires.

Parallel realities can exist, all you have to do is allow them to do so. The world was completed the moment it was created. Everything already existed; even the things that don't exist yet will do so in time. We are not creating anything new which is not already in the mind of the universe, but we are creating a new relationship with these realities.

So how long in linear time do these new realities take to form? The answer is the time you take to believe you are the co-creator and commit to dedicating yourself to improving your level of existence. If you can't imagine your worth, how can the universe know it?

As I say throughout this book, you are at the receiving end of all creation All of the universe is an echo of your own request. There is a reason for our *'can't be bothered'* attitude; it derives from a lack of self-love. A person who loves themself is interested in their own well-being.

Your first step to imagining a better life for yourself is to love the life you have. As we consciously and intentionally love ourselves, love will inspire your thoughts and visions. We can't imagine great things for ourselves if we don't believe we are worthy. Anything we can conceive through imagination can be achieved. But, like positive self-talk, your subconscious mind will only accept your request to process the imagination you place in front of it when belief is involved. Faith can move mountains. When you know, you create your own reality. When you have complete faith in yourself it becomes the most powerful energy that we, as humans, possess. When you know this you will have no doubts. This certainty has been experienced by very few, but the ones who know they are solely their own creators achieve what others only hope for.

Whatever we focus our attention on expands and creates a reality in our lives. Many people have created miracles in their life due to the fact of them having a natural ability to use their insight and imagination to both create and resolve circumstances.

The law of creation is always working through you; changing your focus of attention is not an easy thing to do when coming from a negative mind-set full of self-doubt and self-criticism. Vivid imaginations with the worst outcome are most common in a person who is not aware of their true inner-self. When your mind is taken over with worry and fear, use this spiritual practice of visualisation to get your mind working for you, and not against you. Your state of mind belongs to you and no one else. The more you visualise a good outcome, the easier it will become to achieve.

Although there is a blessing in our fears, worries, and concerns, negative imaginations take longer to materialise due to the fact that the low energy vibration frequencies have a low magnetic power with which to manifest your reality. Thank God, for who knows what kind of monsters would come knocking at our door! Love on the other hand, has a high magnetic pulling power – the energies and vibrations are much more powerful receptors for the creation of life's manifestations.

If you ask anyone on a busy high street what are their goals, and what they want out of life you will most likely be greeted with a blank stare of confusion. This is due to the fact that the world has told people to look outside of themselves for the quest of happiness and self-fulfilment. I absolutely do not believe we attract exactly what we want for most of the time because we are preconditioned to want and desire things that the world has dictated to us, such as saying we need certain things to make us feel better about ourselves. I think that is one of the biggest cons going: the system that keeps you buying in the hope of finding happiness. It keeps you insecure and searching for more. I do believe we can attract the exact situations we need to grow and evolve as beings of humanity. The law of creation works every time but we must not mistake positive thinking with wishful thinking; if we do we replace our real life with a falsity of simply wishing things would change. Life is all about action, and action is all about how much we think we are worth in putting the effort into changing our lives.

As we become self-loving we become more authentic and sincere in our requests. In short, we start to realise what is most important to us. If your request is genuine it will always manifest in essence what you truly desire. True visualisation works only if love is the driving force behind it. If you visualise without loving, you will achieve very little by way of what you want. People have wasted an entire life chasing futile dreams and notions that one day they will land that dream job or they will become famous, richer, smarter, admired. Vanity should be left in the hands of those who merely want to chase their life away.

Material gain isn't the answer; what humans are looking for is feeling good about themselves. This experience of our true self outweighs these external pleasures which are always short-lived and fleeting in nature.

Use the power in you to see your life take flight. See, believe and achieve. Visualise yourself in love, in peace, and in an abundance of joy.

This is the greatest gift you can give yourself – make your first goal to love. As we gain clarity we gain vision in what we truly need. Become authentic and sincere with your true desires and love will keep the vision – your mission, alive until its seed has manifested itself with abundance.

I once had a thousand goals but now my only goal is to love in a thousand ways. I made love a priority first inside myself, and then to take it out into the world. My goals became singular which affected my life in a multitude of ways.

True desires should excite you a lot and fear you little indicating that your desires are in alignment with your higher-self – your soul's desires. Goals are essential for your growth. You came here to evolve; human beings find fulfilment in personal growth, in fact your soul's purpose is to know itself through you. That can be said to be the ultimate goal of the universe.

So, love first, and then follow on only with material goals of your careful choosing. Love will ignite the passion back into your life through your imagination. I tell people who want to visualise material manifestations of any kind i.e. financial stability, improved health, new partners , etc., to make sure what they truly desire excites them with love. It is like having a large bank account with love being the currency you exchange for goods.

I love using visualisation for one reason only – to see myself loved, happy and abundantly fulfilled. To imagine anything good in life requires first to imagine the good in yourself. Nothing can prevent this picture from coming into concrete form except the same power which gave it birth – yourself.

Visualisation Guide.

1. *Close your eyes and move into a comfortable position.*
2. *Think what you desire for a happy loving environment.*
3. *Make it into a scene.*

4. Evoke all your senses.

5. Focus on detail.

6. Repeat until your feelings resonate with the image.

Spiritual Practice 6: *Be Thankful*

Where there is love there is more. The irony to life is the more you have the more you attract. Having an attitude of gratitude promotes abundance in your life, for the law of creation can only manifest more of what you are. Gratitude is an act of kindness we can allow ourselves to perform; it re-aligns us back into the flow of true happiness. We then become grateful for what we have. Life becomes an amazing journey. What you are is the beginning of something great. Gratitude gives you a fresh start like being born again. Everything changes when we are grateful; from personal relationships to your monetary situations. A dull and lifeless relationship can instantly flourish by seeing the good in another rather than complaining about what is wrong with them. And if we are grateful for the money we have, however little, we will see our money magically grow. Change your attitude and you will change your life.

Remember, it is not joy that makes us grateful but rather it is gratefulness that makes us joyful. Expressing gratitude shifts your output of energy; it puts you in harmony with your source of supply so that the good in everything moves towards you. When you are grateful you attract more good things to be grateful for. Take gratitude very seriously if you want to joyously experience a dynamic life. I never leave the house without thanking my bed for the good night's sleep, my cell phone that keeps me In touch with my loved ones, the clothes that I am dressed in, and the breakfast that I enjoyed eating.

A simple spiritual practice is to count your blessings. This practice will raise your vibrational frequency. As you are praising and blessing you are experiencing the highest frequency of love. It simply makes you feel good, and that in turn attracts more good.

Start to observe objects that you use daily, like your computer or the car you drive, and say thank you to those objects. Put love back into everything. The more you do this the more love will reflect back to you, as we realise how these incredible objects benefit our lives. Every object has energy, and the more we thank and bless every single thing we use, have, and own, the more we receive from them. Make a place for love to return to every single thing you do and have, and more shall be added. Blessing everything in your life ignites the law of creation into powerful action. When gratitude becomes an essential foundation in our lives miracles start to appear everywhere.

As the great, late, *Dr. Wayne Dyer* said:

'Deficiency motivation doesn't work. It will lead to a life-long pursuit of try to fix me. Learn to appreciate what you have and where and who you are.'

There are two sides to thanksgiving, one is being thankful for what one has, the second is being self-aware that you are the co-creator of life itself.

A truly thankful heart is one that is full of appreciation of the divinity and sacredness they behold within themselves. If the heart is not full, the soul is empty. If your daily life is not touched by some kind of appreciation for just the fact you are alive. It can be said that you are spiritually dead already. Appreciate the fact you're still breathing, see the blessing in the moment your feet touch the ground every morning. This is more than enough to be grateful for.

Life responds to your every thought, word, and deed. Ironically the things in life that are free are the things that make us most content. Love, compassion, and kindness, are some of things in abundance to be grateful for. As you begin to become aware of the abundance of love within you, the list of things will continue to grow and grow. Be thankful.

There is a special power that lies in gratitude: When you show gratitude more things are presented to you to be grateful for.

You are the only one that can give your life true meaning with peace and joy. If you have not found appreciation in what you are doing, you are looking in the wrong direction for the truth of a life of self-fulfilment.

What are you looking for? Why are you still unhappy? Why can't you seem to appreciate life's little miracles... they are all around you. When will it be the right time to just say thank you for being alive?

When life seems to be against you, the answer is this: Life isn't against you. Rather you are against yourself. The answer to a merry and peaceful life is to be merry and peaceful in your own life. Change your self-perception and life will change in harmony with what you are. True appreciation comes only when you have harnessed love and tasted this divinity for yourself. Nothing can compare to love. Songs have been sung about it, movies have re-enacted it. Love has eluded humans from the very beginning of time. As soon as you return to love you will feel an immediate sense of deep connection with all creation; you will feel the true meaning of compassion, kindness, and integrity, for they have never gone out of fashion. You will appreciate the beauty and abundance around you like never before. The awakening process allows you to enjoy your life without being consumed by your goods. You will instinctively know you are the gift of life itself, and what comes with this appreciation is a self-realisation of knowing that love created this beautiful thing we call life.

Spiritual Practice 7: *Solitude*

Solitude is vital in the return to love to enable yourself to hear your own inner wisdom. In moments of silence and solitude you become self-aware. This inner awareness shows us a way of communicating with your higher self – love. Solutions and ideas always seem to come when a certain amount of distraction of the world's noise is tamed. In that gap of opportunity, the mind can become still. It takes no more than five minutes or so to shut down, come away from the world, and give yourself space away from you phone, computer, or television.

Breath, and just be quiet. This will dramatically increase your well-being. A true intelligence is found in a place of the mind that is away from opinions and judgments. Why do you think Jesus entered the desert for forty days and nights? He knew the commotions of the world would distract him from himself.

When you intentionally enter solitude you cultivate a sixth sense. Your hearing will become acute to the voice of the soul through the stillness and silence of your inner-self. You will be able to hear yourself inside out; the soft whisper of your inner voice will be unlike the chatter box of the mind. It will be motivating, encouraging, and supporting with a generous helping of general good feeling, of certainty and inspiration. You will know the difference between the soul's true guidance and the basic reactive instructions from your mind.

* * * * *

These *Spiritual Practices* need to become part of your daily life. We need to deliberately live our lives the way we consciously choose to live them. Never forget to love ourselves in the absence of judgment and in the presences of positive self-talk and creative imagination. And last, but certainly not least, by being grateful of having this opportunity to be alive, we will successfully experience what it means to be a dynamic human being.

<u>Always remember the universal power of saying these words;</u>

THANK YOU.

CHAPTER 4: A RETURN TO LOVE IN THE PRESENT MOMENT

Life that is scripted is boring, it leaves the individual in a dull and empty void. Instead, life should be random, organic, and spontaneous in nature; life is about feeing alive.

At this very moment you are alive; you are breathing, and if you are already experiencing a return to love through this book, then you are most likely witnessing the love that is radiating from inside of you. Life can never be divided into past and future. The reality is that this is another concept formed by the ego to keep us incarcerated by the illusion the past has gone, the future is yet to come. This present moment is the most powerful place to be, for it is the only true place. Your life may seem to be separated into past and future, but this can't be. You can remember the past and think about the future now, but as reality goes they have no real power. The past is usually a place we miss or regret, the future is usually a tense that we either get very excited or fearful about. This way of behaving wastes vital energy that depletes our life force within. As we focus our attention on the present, you will find that you will be free of negative thought, but still highly alert. The more aware you become of the present, the more things become real and help us to diminish the phantom ego. The very fact that we are not thinking about the past or future dissolves the negativity within the mind and prevents it from taking over. The power of *now* transforms your thinking, thus stopping you from following the belief that the past can define you, and that your future will save you. Just because a large proportion of the population has adopted this belief system it does not mean that it is not insane. Something happens when you begin to live your life to the full, it has an air of freshness and newness to it. Humans get bored, not because life is boring, but because they are bored of the repetitive belief system they have been subjected to. An infinite being announces itself to us when we are merely present in life. This brings about a new consciousness where life is being realised by the individual at that very moment. Love can never be seen, but it can always be felt through self-awareness. This is where peace, joy, and love can be found. Answer this: Has there ever been a time when you are not living in the present moment? Does the past still exist now? Have you ever experienced the future in the present moment? Remember this: living, loving and being in the present moment, is the only true power of reality there is. What you are experiencing now is creating the instantaneous moment that paves the way for the next chapter of your life. However, this moment presents challenges because you can find yourself lost in both discontentment and resentment of the past, and of worrying about the future. But remember – neither the past or future can disturb your peace of mind. When you find yourself lost, explore the reason why you are lost. If you feel that you should be further along in your life, and hold a perception that you should be somewhere other than where you are now, then you will be lost in anxiety and stress. If this frustrates you, then use this anger to motivate you to change and take action. If you feel that something is holding you back, then remember to look for your place in the world and act upon it.

One thing that I do not believe in is fate. The idea that your life has a purpose or plan is wrong. How you live your life is how you choose to live, and not by something that was decided for you from the moment your soul existed. You could say that your life is a map, but it can be rewritten at any time. Real power is not about controlling your life but merely allowing it to unfold in the realisation that you will find yourself taking journeys you would have never thought of participating in. Here is a helpful hint: the path you always fear is the correct path to take. What you are afraid to do is a clear indication of the next thing you need to do. The other side of fear is growth. Remember, without new experiences something inside us falls asleep.

The reason for your frustration is because you are placing value on the wrong things in life. These unrealistic expectations such as finding life-long love by the time you are 21, or being a multi-millionaire by 40 are causing you frustration. But if we look closer at our lives it is really the expectations of other people that cause your anxiety. We put so much pressure on ourselves by attaching importance to the way the world sees us, but the sooner you value and listen to your internal clock, the happier you will become. You will find love when it happens, you will marry when the time is right, and if you want to, have children when you feel you should. Take a gap year if you don't want to go to university, pursue a passion or dream; don't be shy, be your true self. This is *your* life.

Do not listen to other people's expectations of you. Become whoever you need to be. One helpful tip might be to self-reflect: Ask yourself, do you feel you are where you should be in your career or love life by now? If not, do you think you are behind because of the expectations of yourself, or of others? Just remember, the moment you allow yourself to accept where you are in life is the moment you begin to truly live it. The more you want to be somewhere else the more you push life further away. This moment is where you are, it has peace, a purpose, and a promise. You are an amazing human being regardless of where you find yourself. Whatever position you hold in life you are of irreplaceable value. True self-worth doesn't come from what we have, but from who we are and if we can't accept ourselves without conditioning then we will never experience the true intent our life holds for us. Here is exactly where love and peace can be found, but you must be bold. Don't be told how, when and where to live your life, make your decisions... do it now. The past and the future keep the presence of love hidden. When you are willing to let go of yesterday's happening's and tomorrow's worries, you will instantly be provided with peace of mind. If the truth be known, it is the peace from your own ego that is revealed. When we simply stop worrying and focus on the present moment, we find life becomes easier.

To love is to be in the presence of one's self. Your emotions are not what they seem to be, they are part of the illusion of the past and future. Your true feelings can only be felt in the gap between the past and the future. Feelings of love, peace, joy, courage, strength, and wisdom, become our reality when we are truly living in the present. Eureka moments are not realised yesterday or tomorrow but today. If you need to make a decision of any kind, go also towards the situation with your gut feelings, not only with your head. The mind will always present solutions and ideas when we are simply in that process of moment by moment reality. Insight comes not before but when we are focusing on the present moment. If you had one minute left to make a decision that would either cause you life or death, you would always be more insightful there would be no *'maybe'*, your actions would be precise and certain. The intensity in that present moment would be right every time. The power which is known to us when we are merely present in our life is amazing. Remember, there is no time like the present to make good decisions, once you spend less time pondering on things that don't serve this moment, the clearer life becomes. Don't wait for the future to become who you want to be, take action and live now, always see your preferred state of being now, for that's what the future holds for you.

The present is all you need to orchestrate the rest of your life. To remember anything but the sacredness of your sheer inner beauty is useless information that will hold you back in a world of fear. Pain and pleasure are a conundrum; the reflection of the past and the future. The space between is where you will find peace and joy in the moment of the present time. There is a fine line between reality and what we perceive to be real in our lives; one gives you joy and peace when you can truly accept it, the other may send you pleasurable experiences, but if you are not at peace with your present life looking to the future will always leave you with a sense that something is missing. What needs to happen is quite simple: remove that deep concept within you of time having an effect on how you lead your life by loving fearlessly and unconditionally. Reality and peace go hand in hand.

So, what is this reality? Your reality can never be experienced other than from the point of where you are *now*. It will remain dormant until you awaken it. Your love for yourself is unseen, the reality that is you – your self-awareness, is the key. The practice of living in a way that means you become fully aware of yourself is something you can do now – and all of the time, every moment of every day. When you are not living your life with full self-awareness you are not practising love; you are worrying... and worry is a sure sign that your mind is trained elsewhere.

Remember this: once you truly live in the present moment you spend less time pondering or questioning things that don't serve that moment. Accept and respect yourself exactly as you are now, don't wait for the future to become who you wish to be. I waited a long time for this gift of life then one day I realised that I was that gift; I was my own touch paper – I just needed lighting.

Most people die inside a long time before they are buried, but you have the power to change your life in an instant. I hear you ask how can I suddenly change to live my life this way completely right now? I have so much to do; my job, commitments, my partner, my family, money concerns... they all need my attention. These things cause suppression and depression and so you become stressed, feeling the world is always on your shoulders. For you to be the best you can be for your family and loved ones, to be able to make a successful career and fulfil all your commitments, you must become the person without preoccupation; your true self. The quality of your future hangs in the balance of the quality of this moment. Your consciousness of love has to be deliberate, if it isn't you will never fully experience the wonders of your soul's purpose. Even though the presence of love is in you, you must activate it. You must give it self-recognition now and at all times. Of course, always focus on where you want to go, but never forget where you are now; remember, life is about balance.

If you stay the same, then changing your job, partner, the place you live, won't make any difference. When you change yourself then everything around you changes and the only space where that change can happen is in *you*. Show up in your life, be your own self-expression, hear yourself speak, laugh, and listen to yourself. Observe how you walk, how you drive your car, how you dress, undress, eat, drink... the list is endless, just be sure to know yourself. Catch yourself at every moment where most people are not even aware that they are even alive. They have become numb – desensitised by the constant demand of their own minds. They are always looking for the next best thing. Living for real in the present will add so much vitality and energy to your life, don't expect there to be something going on all the time, that's such an unrealistic expectation. The world is not always exciting, dynamic and enthralling, but you are when you live love and breathe now. Preserve your life energy for when you need to fully express yourself in the world. When you honour that life force of love within you by simply just being, you will achieve more in life.

Until you become fully self-aware you will not realise you have a constant companion in your head. The constant chatter of the mind is predominantly negative and destructive and depletes your energy. Through self-observation a miracle happens: the mind pauses for you to reclaim your true self from the incarceration it has suffered. An enormous amount of energy goes into being negative, this energy is released back into the body. When you can truly be present... and I mean really understand, cherish and love the present moment, it is a gift. Then, and only then, can you become a force of calm over the madness of the world. By doing this you start to become grounded in the force of the moment, and when that happens, you become free of all the negativity served up by the mind.

Live your life *now*. Love yourself *now*. Accept yourself *now*. Respect yourself now. You will stand the test of time, for time is the illusion.

'Love, and do what you will '

St. Augustine of Hippo

What is more beautiful than this?

Applying the following *Spiritual Practices* will help you in a return to love in the present moment: *'Choice is a simple decision'* , *'First: Love Yourself'* , *'Self-talk'* , *'Imagination and Visualisation'*.

CHAPTER 5: A RETURN TO LOVE IN RELATIONSHIPS

There are so many facets that come into play when we talk about a real return to love so I have headed them into groups for further discussion.

Sexuality and relationships: Love has no sexuality. It is neither heterosexual, bi-sexual, homosexual, or cross-gender. Our sexuality is defined outside of the labels given by the institutions of the world that exist to categorise, segregate, and irrationalise love. Yes, it can be said one's sexual orientation is an attraction towards a certain sex, but it can't ultimately define who we truly are. True self-love pierces through any barriers of gender.

Love cannot define love by comparison to anything or anyone, or in anyway. You can't physically hold love, or put it in a bottle and label it; love has no prioritisation. Anybody telling you that you are wrong for loving another human being is a person who truly doesn't know the meaning of love. Show compassion and humility for the ignorance of your fellow man who has forgotten who they truly are. If the truth be known the false sense of self/ego has no other way to define itself other than through the condemnation of another.

Alone in love: What about if you are alone, how do you return to love without another's reflection? If you find yourself alone, (which in truth you never are), remember you can never feel more alive than when you are completely yourself. In fact, when a person is living alone they are as likely to harness love as with living with a partner. As long as it is by choice and you are not holding on to fears of being hurt or rejected, being alone in love can help you. The advantage of being alone by choice is that there are less distractions to gain your attention. You will have time to build the relationship with yourself to discover who you truly are so when and if you choose to find a new partner, you will be ready.

Being alone doesn't mean being lonely. In fact, just because someone is in a relationship doesn't mean they don't feel personally alone. Loneliness can be felt even more deeply if someone around you is incapable of expressing their love and feelings towards you.

A lack of physical and mental affection towards another is nothing less than emotional neglect. That being said, the worst kind of loneliness is a negation of self-love. Humans have a deep yearning for love and affection and at some point in your life you will experience a disconnection with those around you. Sometimes this disconnection can be justified by how someone is treating you, but very often this feeling of isolation comes from your own barriers, from the walls you have built around yourself. Our infinite souls require two versions of the same thing; a remembrance of our own love, and a reminder of the love that is in the reflection of another. Loneliness is caused by the forgetting of our own love. The answer to finding a loving connection with people around you is to first have that unity with yourself.

Feel your own feelings: If you are in a relationship and are feeling a lack of attention, then address that feeling within yourself first. Ask yourself how you can give yourself more of what you need right now at this very moment? By reversing the act of wanting attention from another you claim your love back. The return to love has a dramatic effect especially in co-dependency relationships. Whenever you are harnessing love you will become clearer about your own needs of what makes YOU a happier human being. Our needs are very different, we are all unique in our quest for life. When you face whatever you feel is missing within the relationship, face it without projecting your own feelings emotions and insecurities. It is okay to be lonely, annoyed and frustrated, as long as you process it all through self-acknowledgement of your own feelings; don't hold your partner accountable for the emotions you are feeling. Then, and only then, can real change begin to happen. True openness will always bring you back. Strength can always be found when taking a situation at face value. Face your partner in a none-judgmental way, tell them your true feelings; honour your own feelings.

Both passive and aggressive behaviours are common in any normal day to day relationship, but playing victim serves no one, it shows a lack of reverence which always leads to further pain and suffering. Be interested and aware of what is happening inside of you rather than always projecting what is happening outside of you. Avoidance solves nothing. When you come from a position of truth and sincerity a true open communication is possible between two people, this truth never hurts as much as the denial of one's true feelings. In all relationships we communicate simultaneously on at least two levels: what we say, which is always a communication of how you feel, and what we do. Be sure your communication is consistent for actions will always represent true feelings, and actions speak louder than words.

Love breaks down barriers and builds up a channel of sublime communication, so go beyond your fears... if someone truly loves you they will be waiting for you there. Always be true to yourself. Being truthful means accepting your weaknesses and building on your strengths.

Be a Romantic: Now if you find yourself wanting a partner the question you must first ask yourself is not, *what do I want out of a relationship?* But more; *What do I have to give?* So often people dive into new relationships thinking it's going to save them from a dull and boring existence. No one is coming to save you and make your life amazing and exciting if you don't recognise within you how amazing and exciting you already are. Be perfectly honest with yourself about being ready to date and share your love and life with another person; being emotionally available is vital when entering a new relationship, and emotional baggage of any kind will flaw it from the very beginning. Your past relationships will come back to haunt you time and time again if you haven't moved on mentally and emotionally. It is unkind and unfaithful to date another person when you are still affected by your past.

As I have said, be really honest with yourself, ask yourself if you are a person you would date? Are you exciting and interesting? Would you want to live with you? Don't be surprised if all the answers to these self-provocations are negative... this is the whole purpose of the journey in the return to love. As long as you feel unlovable or unworthy you will unconsciously sabotage yourself. You cannot heal a lifetime of pain overnight, be patient and kind to yourself, it takes as long as it takes to rebuild yourself, but love is instant when the moment of focus on your life in this way occurs. Self-awareness is all you need to find your appropriate mate, so don't hide from your flaws, embrace them, know them and accept them and they will change. Owning your flaws is self-empowering. I had a client who thought he was ready for a romantic relationship. After a lengthy discussion we both came to the conclusion he wanted someone to give him the excitement and the thrill that he couldn't find and had denied himself. We set a love programme for him to follow. It included a list of qualities he was seeking in a potential life-long partner. After reading the list together I asked him to apply this assessment to himself, wearing the shoes of the other person. Through persistence of imagining, loving, and speaking positively about himself, he started to like himself. A month went by and he was invited to a barbecue that originally hadn't been in his plans, and he met his now partner. We can only ever have that what we are being and expressing; the law is absolute on this matter.

Find yourself: If you have become single after a long-term relationship it would be wise to now explore who you really are. This is the time to heal and become you again. Rediscover your own interests and passions. Travel – see new places, meet new people while you start to live life again through self-awareness. Life will present itself to you in ways you could have never have imagined. Being broken isn't the worst place to be. The lessons in life are there to make you, not break you. Until you recognise the greatness in you hold within yourself, you will always be making your choice from a place of weakness.

Spiritual Practices 'Choice is a simple decision', and 'First: Love yourself' might help you with this.

Is fear of being hurt stopping you moving into a new relationship?

It is better to have loved and lost than never to have loved at all. Love hurts sometimes, not because love itself can actually hurt us, but the lack of it does.

If you have been single for a while and are afraid of commitment this is a sure sign of holding on to the past. The key is always to learn from the past and let it go. Life's journey is too short for us to dwell on what he or she or even you yourself did. Whatever happened in the past should always remain in the past. Move on in love and it will show you the way to trust again. More importantly, trust yourself. As humans have a tendency to mess things up and hurt people along the way, the more you know yourself the less you will become affected by the antics of others and will therefore be able to avoid any part of it. This is where your true inner strength lies and no one can diminish it. The mind always has that voice of doubt that says *don't love, you will get hurt,* but truth be known, if you don't love everyone, you will get hurt. Believe in love again, by first believing in yourself.

The biggest miss-carriage of justice is for us to say we are not good enough to be loved. It is so sad to see this crime of humanity causing so much pain and a poverty of love in the world. The loveless are roaming the earth in search of themselves, and the world has taught them they are not good enough. Forgive these teachings, these values, beliefs and doctrines by going beyond this. Remember, no one can show you love before you show it to yourself. Keep working on harnessing love and this illusionary narrative will leave you, then, you can go on to experience love in its greatest form.

The world is full of amazing good people waiting to meet you, there is no shortage of supply of love, you just have to be emotionally available, which always means being honest with yourself. Love is always readily at hand for the person whom is ready to cultivate it. None of us are perfect; you are not alone. We are all broken in some way, so waiting for your perfect partner is a mantra that shouldn't be chanted. It is a deep conceptual belief that seeking the perfect person will one day save you from your imperfections. This is no more than the belief that you are not worthy of being loved. If you never see yourself as good enough you will never find a partner good enough for you. Your unrealistic expectations of another will always make you fall short in the love making process; this is why so many are stuck in the *'seek and never find'* mode. It is all to do with fear. There are an unprecedented amount of people living alone, not by choice but from fear of being hurt. I'm not saying everyone who is single is lonely and not everyone who is taken is truly in love, but humans have a deep yearning for love and connection with each other, this has never changed and cannot be changed.

There is no going back in the law of creation. It can be said that a purpose of humanity is to remind each other of our greatness not our weakness, and in doing so we remember ourselves. Humans need each other to make each other happy. Yes, having all your desires filled without someone to share that sunset with leaves a void; love needs love to know itself, life is to be shared not spared.

When you come to know the love within you as truth you will have awoken your true self. Knowing the truth of who you are will initiate only one goal in your life, and it will be not how to find love, but rather how to share and express it. You will know when you are ready to date and be in a relationship because although content with being alone, you will feel so much love inside you that the need to express it will become overwhelming.

At the best of times when true love is present, you will find that you don't need to go looking for a partner, they will seem to just find you. This happens when you get on with your life and in that space, nothing is missing. You feel good and complete in your endeavours. The irony of life is that when you don't need anything, everything appears. When this happens it is always for your highest good. Your future mate will always come gift-wrapped and appear at the most random moment; the least expected is the most effective. As you live your life intentionally through self-love you will feel the presence of goodness in you. This is the ingredient that draws the right people and circumstance of situation to you. Once you feel good, things come to you, it really is as simple as that. Love makes you attractable, you will be like a magnet, for love makes you more attractive and its very beauty is seductive and highly sexually appealing.

I tell people, if you are single and choose to date, give up on being perfect and begin the work of becoming yourself through self-love and self-acceptance. Those two qualities will bring about a self-awareness that will tell you the person you meet is lucky to meet you because of just how amazing you are. Action through the fullness of love instead of the fear of scarcity of love is so much more intuitive and productive; keep your heart open. Compatible traits and behaviours often emerge shortly after you have decided to date, you may never have noticed them before. Listen to your feelings and those whispers from the universe within you, they will guide you to your soul mate.

Being in a relationship: If you are in a relationship you can harness love together in a beautiful way, deepening your love for one another and reminding each other of the sacred love you both hold. The purpose of any relationship is to grow in love together and keep witnessing this love as the true testimony. I believe all relationships can pass the test of time if both parties can respect each other's boundaries as individuals while being a couple. Losing your self-identity is a sure way to cause unhappiness within the relationship. When fear of not being good enough represents itself within the relationship through judgments criticism and blame, be an observer of the insecurities that arise between you both. Learn to listen before you respond, don't try to fix them through judgments or convictions. In a relationship we grow far quicker through the reflections of others because your partner will always reflect back to you what you cannot or will not see in yourself.

The illusion is that relationships will take away pain and insecurities, the reality is that relationships magnify them; fears issues and insecurities are so hidden in one's self that only through another are they made apparent. Fears or resentment might show up in the mirror image of you partner through judgments or criticisms, but if we look closer you will see part of yourself in that judgment. Whatever you believe to be true of yourself will always be reflected through another. The beauty in the beast nevertheless is always on holy ground – to love and heal that part of you that needs more love and acceptance.

Self-empowerment always comes from you. The behaviour of others is not in your control but your behaviour always is. Be mindful; learning to assert yourself starts by understanding that you are not trying to control what other people do, but rather you are controlling your own actions and feelings. Reclaim your self-dignity, you are worth that at least. By speaking about what you are feeling with your partner gives them more chance of understanding both you and themselves. This will allow your true love for each other to grow. A true relationship contains clashes of opinions, tugs of war, tears for fears, but most of all a friend who can forgive them all.

Deliberately see the good in your partner, try to follow what I have said to bring the best out of each other. Don't wait for your partner to join you in love, we are all evolving at different rates so don't be concerned with their actions or non-actions in the process of becoming a love-maker. Show them the way, and lead by example.

Be a witness not a judge. Focus on yourself, not others. Nothing anyone can say can really define you be it positive or negative. It will all become irrelevant and insignificant when your self-worth is based on who you are instead of the opinions of others. You are free from the nonsense of the world when you don't need the world to define you. Of course, it matters what people think about us, especially our partners, friends and loved ones, they will have many valid points and can in many cases be the ignition for us to make a real success out of our lives. Behind a great man is a great woman to motivate him, but we must remember that self-love, self-worth, and self-respect starts and ends with you. Words and actions of others are not able to describe the true essence of your greatness. Focus on loving yourself instead of loving the idea of other people loving you.

The Spiritual Practice: 'Never Judge Yourself' will help to ground your daily actions towards being a witness and never a judge.

Love needs no defending or protection of its grace. Through loving yourself you will know how to love another and show each other the utmost respect and kindness. Remind each other how great you both are, ignite the fire and passion that is in you both. Two logs always burn stronger together, so stop waiting for the relationship to be perfect before you start having real intimacy. It makes no sense at all to wait for something you already have, if it's not going to be now for you to experience love when will it be? Keep your relationship fresh, exciting, and new by merely giving it pure attention and love. Couples can't rely on memories alone; if you don't show up in your relationship it is likely to fail.

Relationships will always have polar opposites, sometimes you will feel disconnected or even unhappy with your partner and they will feel the same towards you, this disconnectedness is due to the loss of the sense of self and the forgetfulness of our true nature. Sometimes you will need to lead the relationship and other times your partner will lead you back to love. This is a perfectly normal and safe pattern in an environment where two people love each other. The problem comes when love is not being reciprocated. A withdrawal of love is felt so deeply within a person whose reflection of love is not being received. As I said, love doesn't need another to love, it needs only to feel its own essence returned through another. This breakdown in connection can be a very painful experience, especially after a long relationship where love can become stagnated through complacency and familiarity.

The more your sense of self depends on approval of others the more likely you are to be blind of the warning signs way ahead. This is so often seen in new relationships – jumping in too deep and to fast. This will sometimes make you regret the long-term consequence of being in a relationship that just isn't right for you. Your sense of self-love can never be diminished because someone has rejected your love through the demonstration of unkind words, actions or a withdrawal of love towards you. If this is what you are going through give yourself time and space to heal; remember your self-expression always creates your own experiences in life, that's why it is important to let go of the feeling that other people are the cause of your unhappiness and your insecurities. Stop trying to make them be what you want them to be in order for you to be content. Prioritise your own needs if they are not being met, and never forget, if someone has left you for no apparent reason it is their loss, not yours.

It could be that you have lost feelings for someone: Personalising these emotions as self-guilt or self-blame will not allow you to understand your feelings further. It has been said that if a relationship is failing, then if you really love someone you will let them go. This is hard to comprehend, but if you take a closer look the purpose of love is to express its joy, peace and unity. If you are feeling none of these qualities for your partner, and if they are truthful with themselves, then they will be feeling it too. You and they, just like everyone else are reflections of one another. Whatever the reasons of the disharmony within yourself, be honest, and then everything else will fall into place.

The Death of a Relationship: There is an old Italian saying my mum always says:

'Rather be alone than in bad company.'

I love myself and am willing to release the need for relationships that don't nourish and support me. Relationships don't usually end instantly, they die slowly. When unresolved hurt and anger are left. Issues of untrustworthiness, withdrawal of love, and no ability to show commitment will inevitably mean that the life span of the relationship is limited. For two people to stay together after the trust has gone is futile, but it is the most difficult thing to make that decision to stay or go. Prolonging your misery only causes you loss of self-worthiness, respect and compassion towards yourself. Always gather your thoughts in any uncertain situation, love yourself enough to trust yourself, be ready to release them if your relationship is dying; it makes no sense to delay the inevitable. Do not hang on to anyone for the false sake of thinking you should, you will always have someone in your life, but they must be there as love.

Rejection of love: Rejection is always a reflection of the other person's capability of authenticism and compassion to show their true feelings about themselves. This shown lack of love is always a lack of respect they hold within a conceptual thought about themselves. It is so sad to see how humans can behave awfully towards one another because they have forgotten how to love. The constant fear of not feeling good enough often causes them to act cruelly. Rejection of another always represents a fear of commitment for anyone. We all know feelings change, but it is part of life – to make a commitment. Be honest and authentic with everyone.

If someone walks away without trying it would indicate they were waiting for an excuse to leave anyway, Judging anyone else's flaws becomes your flaw. Deep seeded insecurities, a lack of trust and commitment, or rejection, is not a true reflection of you, rather it is of them. No one can actually reject our love because we are love. You can never lose what you are. Uphold your sense of self-respect it is your upmost truth; never allow the behaviour of others to define the sacredness and beauty that is you.

If your heart has been broken through the ending of a relationship, always remember, the purpose of a broken heart is to allow the love to break through and embrace you with compassion, kindness, and tenderness. When a loss of any kind disturbs your life you will find you are never more yourself than in those moments of pure heartbreak and vulnerability. The tears you bleed are the soul's holy water washing your pain away. Never forget the love you shared was never conclusive, to have loved and be loved will be the only truth that remains long after the relationship has ended. Love is the only thing that is real, and for that very reason it never perishes. However your relationship ended never really matters in the end, unresolved hurt and anger are always left with the person who is holding on to them, so always remember to wish your ex-partner well. One thing you must never forget is to forgive. Forgiving others releases us from the disturbances others have caused us. As I have said, the easiest way to find inner peace is to stop judging yourself and others, if you don't trust and forgive people, it means you haven't let go of the past. Life is too short to hang on to vindictive grudges. Realise that the value of a person is always more important than the value of their mistakes. What people do are often not true representations of their true nature; humans become broken through not loving and not knowing themselves. We will always make mistakes and pay the consequences as it is our thoughts and actions that dictate our reality. Until you replace fear with love these problems just keep reoccurring. Like all problems, relationship issues of any kind always come down to a dissociation with your true self. The quality of your life always depends upon the quality of your relationships with others, and this always depends on the relationship you have with yourself.

The relationship between you and your true self is the catalyst for having amazing relationships with the whole of humanity.

When you have connected with that sacred space of love inside yourself, you will feel the connection within every relationship you encounter, for the unseen bond that you and I share is of the one love.

The Spiritual Practice: 'First: Love Yourself' will help you apply this self-love.

1. To love anyone, you must love yourself first, so be your first concern. Once you do your life will improve. This doesn't mean you don't have concerns for your loved ones, but your concerns will be in balance with everyone's needs.

2. Love without expectation. True love is not a means to an end but the end itself.

3. If you are alone and wishing to meet a soulmate make sure your become attractive. The more love you have the more people will be attracted to that love. Love is seductive.

4. If you feel you are in a loveless relationship, enter love from the point you are now. Any situation is good enough for you to experience love. Focus on loving yourself within the relationship,

your partner can't remain inactive in love if your reflection is only love.

5. Mind your own love, not the love of others.

6. Self–love will give you the love and power to move on, break through the illusionary fear and imprisonment within any relationship

7. Love is the great multiplier, it will turn nothing like itself into itself. There is no corner in the world that it cannot touch or transform.

8. Loving yourself is the only thing you need to remember, then love will remember the rest.

9. Relationships are our sacred learning space.

10. Relationships are the breeding ground to learn about yourself more than to learn about your partner.

11. Give the people in your life space within your space.

    This is unconditional love.

CHAPTER 6: A RETURN TO LOVE IN HEALTH

Our fortuitous well-being and good health can be described as a true gift of life. There's an Italian proverb that says:

'He who enjoys good health is rich, though he knows it not.'

Even a common cold can bring about a self-awareness of appreciation for feeling vibrant and alive once it has passed. The body is an inner reflection of the person. Every negative thought will manifest itself and cause a reaction. When one is stressed, angry, or fearful, these emotions place a physical restriction on the body causing a build-up of toxins which will become a detriment to good health.

A return to love is essential for maintaining balance within the body. It is life's carriage, and is the sacred space within which we meet the love of our own self. No feelings can truly be experienced outside of our body, it is the reflection of the gift of life. It is the visual element of love; a face of an angel outwardly reflects the inner beauty of each of us. Our true natural state of well-being cannot be touched, you can never kill the spirit within the body. When we are truly in touch with ourselves we can harness the power of the full beauty that the love of good health brings. It is not by seeing our body, but by feeling our life within it. If we are lucky enough to live to a ripe old age this will have no effect on the physical changes we might witness. A feeling of being forever twenty-one or at least, young in spirit, will endure. When in our natural state of well-being we are flowing with life. To restore well-being is to reduce fear and increase love in your life. The more that you love the better you will feel, when you are self-aware of the love within you, the negativity that erodes the body can't then cause a reaction leading to ill health. The body is a reflection of you; it can't help but respond to the thoughts you are producing that create the emotions you are feeling. The body needs more than food, exercises and physical processes alone to keep it healthy. What it requires most of all is *your* love and attention for its true inner beauty to be maintained. Until now you may have simply seen your body as something you feed, dress, and become self-obsessed with; you identify it with your age, status, gender, wealth, height and size. There are constant demands being made on our body. Judgments, and criticisms of not being good enough in some way – perhaps not being pretty, slim, rich, clever, or tall enough don't help us. It doesn't matter what these are, they can have a great impact. This causes you to lose sight of your inner beauty and radiance. A constant attack of dissatisfaction can cause fear and make the body weaker, lacking energy and vitality. Symptoms and conditions that can even baffle doctors will quickly develop and appear. Fortunately the medical profession is now finally recognising the connection between these stresses and illnesses developing in the body, and alternative medicine is being offered as an aid back to health. As an example, access to alternative medicine is becoming more wildly available in British hospitals as they are recognising stress as a key contributing factor towards the onset of serious poor health. The pace of our lives has become too fast, we were never meant to live a life crammed full of targets and unrealistic expectations. Social conditioning presents us with systems that are not worth the paper they are written on. The world sells us the lie that there is a constant demand for certain things and that we must chase them so completely. Illness then becomes an inevitable consequence of our quest to become perfect.

Of course, there are many factors that play a part in causing illnesses: the environment, genetics, diet, vices such as drugs, being born with or acquiring a disability, but there is no denying that there is a great connection with the mind's reaction to any of these given circumstances. All negative emotions become merely a reflection of yourself and will eventually display as symptoms of illness. A mere headache can arise because of unnecessary worry about a situation, and when it does so it is the worry that is the underlying problem that has caused the symptom in the first place; therefore the real cure lies in solving just that. It quickly becomes a vicious circle of symptom versus problem. To break the cycle we must challenge the problem either by accepting what is or changing it by taking positive action. Identification is key.

Talking about our ailments keeps them rooted firmly in place because of the law of attraction. The law of attraction is the way in which one's thoughts and attitudes breed a reflection of the same and will therefore always create a like/like situation. So, be very aware of what you are feeling and choose carefully what you say, for broadcasting your every whim is always a negative ploy. Instead, use that same energy to send yourself good vibes. Fuel the body with thoughts of calm acceptance. Put all your attention towards harmonising and balancing your thoughts towards positivity. Love your body and you will find that it will love you back with positive affect. The main reason anyone talks about their health problem is to attract love and attention. The irony is that:

The very thing that so often contributes to our lack of well-being is the very thing humans actually need!

And that is self-love. So often we get this wrong. This lack of love for ourselves comes from the lack of self-awareness and of incompleteness. Just that one negative feeling of not being good enough can cause a multitude of health problems.

If a disease has presented itself through the body, the first thing to do of course is to call your doctor and get medical assistance. Orthodox medicine, especially in the western world is nearly always available to us. Use the medicine as an aid to heal the body but never forget that your spiritual side can often have a far greater effect. While medicine can relieve the symptoms, it is often your inner core that can heal the problem. Allow your mind to think wonderful thoughts – love is the great healer, it is an energy that turns everything unlike itself into itself.

Learn to be the cause of the effect and not the effect of the cause.

Learn to accept what lies in front of you so you can align your thoughts with a solution. There is great talk of fighting illnesses these days and it is true to say we must never give up as long as we have life inside us. There is always hope however serious the situation has become. Don't add to the stress by making a difficult situation worse. If we must fight we must always exercise a degree of love and acceptance. Through that peace we often find the answers that take us towards improving our health.

Being faced with any illness can be a challenging experience, our reactions to worry and fear can be involuntary and it is therefore important to remember that the body is an amazing being in itself, it does most of the work for us: It can heal itself of a mere cut almost overnight, we don't consciously digest our food – it does it for us ... we are not aware of the millions of cells that are being shed every day or that our body has replaced as part of the perpetual healing process. Our interference is a factor that can cause a state of a well-being not to be maintained. We must at least be open and honest about our contribution to this end. The moment you put your focus into your body, which is no more than placing your loving thoughts within yourself, your health will improve. Talk to your body, stand in front of a mirror and tell it you love it. Love your body *especially* when it is in a state of disease.

A daily routine for me is to tell my body how much I appreciate it. I thank my hands for allowing me to do a job, I love and thank my eyes for seeing the wonders of the beauty that surrounds me, and I thank my ears for allowing me to hear the birds in a morning. Bring your body truly alive by giving it your conscious attention. I assure you it will feel and work better for you. Become closer to your body, don't only think in terms on how it looks, but more of how it feels. We are human beings, we respond to basic feelings. The closer you can get to how you really feel the purer you will become and the closer you will get to a fullness of a feeling of well-being.

A quick and easy way to give your body the love and attention it needs is by focusing on your breathing. Intentionally focusing on this can be very beneficial for the rebalancing of well-being within the body.

> **'When the mind is agitated, the breath is agitated.**
> **When the breath is tranquil, the mind is tranquil.'**

The body is always a blue print of the mind, and so calming the mind allows the body to reach a state of peaceful equilibrium. The quality of your breath can actually dictate the quality of your life. This is such a simple truth, breathing is the most natural, autonomous physical operation we perform over which we also have some conscious control. It is our first and our last action in life. As soon as we are born we breathe in, then we breath out. We can practice conscious breathing no matter where we are or what we are doing... and the quality of your breathing can transform your health. Conscious breathing is essentially a process of self-awareness of the life force within our body. It allows us to free ourselves from the chaos and confusions of the mind, and the never ending demands that the world makes of us which contribute to our ill health. It only takes a couple of seconds to grind yourself into this sacred breath.

Sit in a quiet space and stop, focus on your breath, breathe and let life flow in and out. Feel your life force pulsating through your entire body. Remember you are alive, and take time through your day to check in with life itself.

Conscious breathing is a simple spiritual practice that can have massive effect. I invite you to use this process for a couple of minutes a day as often as you can to feel love in its primordial state beyond the familiar conceptual experiences you are used to.

A physician once said that the best medicine for any illness is love. When asked what to do if that doesn't work, he smiled and said... increase the dose.

As you harness self-love, you will feel an increase of energy. This energy is vital for the body's healing process. With the appropriate medical assistances and your application of self-love, the body will heal much faster, without the resistance of the mind's negativity which will hold the healing process back. Forgive yourself for any current disharmony in your life, do it now – today. Then, instead, allow love, patience, acceptance, kindness and compassion to enter your heart and mind. These are all qualities of love, and of a balanced person which will always be reflected outwardly from your body. A healthy mind encourages a healthy body and vice versa. Once you understand and can achieve this state of equilibrium the two become inseparable. Health is a gift of life, it is something you receive each day; be grateful for your health in order to receive more good health. Appreciate and value your life, it is the only one you have:

Take a deep breath... exhale, and say... I Love You – this will

instantly make you feel better.

The Spiritual Practice 'First: Love Yourself' can be applied to the details talked about in this chapter.

CHAPTER 7: A RETURN TO LOVE IN WORK AND MONEY

Fruits of our labour are the reward we seek and can expect. Unless you are lucky enough to gain wealth through the channels of the lucky bonus ball on the lottery, or some kind uncle has left you pots of gold, money will generally be earned by working for it. Our careers are so often windows of self-expression of who we really are; in short, the true purpose of anything we do is to make our values display a worth to the world which fires the mission deep within our soul to evolve, expand and create. We will only find our purpose in life when we apply meaningful reason. If we only see our job of work as means to an end, then the final result will be very unfulfilling indeed; if we are not offering a part of ourselves to the world that includes doing what we love we will never fulfil our true purpose on earth and that is to be of service of others.

We are merely here to serve, inspire, and care for one another. Every industry, every business or enterprise has this one same format that can never be changed. By design, to be of service would achieve nothing without offering that service; from the janitor that cleans the school to the football player who can make his supporters cry by scoring with greatness or losing in despair. Do not delude yourself with grandeurs of ego, we are no more

than service providers. The only difference between what each of us do is in the amount of love we give to it. Behind any successful person there is love. Whatever their skills talents and abilities, nothing in this world would function successfully without there being a passion for one's labour: *love.*

There are countless stories of men and women creating amazing successes through the law of love. They may not have known at the time, but they had the abilities to love their passion, and never give up on their dream which then surfaces as their career. This passion will always face adversities and challenges and is always ridiculed by some, usually those who place their dreams before anything else in life, sacrificing almost everything. But these super powers are fuelled by only one fire – love. They have the natural ability to not take no for an answer, and escape the belief of the curse of scarcity and of not being good enough to achieve their dreams. They believe fearlessly in their love for their craft and become wise, durable, and creatively powerful. All these qualities are within the seed of a successful person who has harnessed the love for their passion. A successful person is not someone with talent but someone with passion, persistence, and perseverance.

To be able to live out your dreams you must understand that if someone has achieved what you truly want to do then let it be proof that it can be achieved. As long as you have enough passion and some skills and talent you can do it. If we lack passion in our life, we lack love, the two are inseparable but of course the reason why we lack passion is because we lack self-worth; not feeling good enough prevents us from achieving our heart's desire. The only reason we remain feeling inferior is because we act in small ways. This damaging belief system has caused the greed which has become a modern-day disease. We believe that we are not automatically entitled to anything, we are not worthy enough. This formula has created a new sort of class system which is based purely on wealth – inferiors, superiors, and a whole lot of doctrines.

The curse of scarcity is not a curse because it isn't true, but because you were told it was whatever you hold to be true for yourself, you shall experience. There is an abundance of true wealth upon this earth, if it were shared throughout the world equally, every person would be very rich indeed. There is more love, beauty, and prosperity than you could encapsulate in a life time. The proof of that are the rich; they have had a natural ability allowing them to tap into the reserves of the universe and to fashion for themselves a creation that is already here. As I have previously explained, creation has already been created – a paradox in itself, but anything you can believe and conceive for yourself you will be able to receive. The lack of something you are experiencing in your life maybe due to circumstances beyond your control i.e. a war-stricken country's natural resources. Governmental restrictions in these circumstances can show the pinnacle of inhumanity, which of course is a lack of love towards their own people.

We only experience a lack of anything in our lives because we don't believe in the natural laws of abundance. A belief in scarcity will prove to you that there is never enough, so will the belief of abundance prove to you that there can always be more than enough? This means your beliefs will always enrich you and become reality if you allow them to.

Love is the only force that can remove a negative mind-set. As I said, we could feed the whole world many times over but the lack of self-awareness of who we truly are obscures this abundance of kindness and compassion. Man's insecurity of not feeling good enough causes such an imbalance to the natural flow of prosperity he derives an endless thirst for wanting more but always feels less.

Greed is the unconscious conceptual belief that you feel you must have more to be more. Believing that there's not enough for everyone including yourself causes a very unkind world. It is the illusion of the bottomless pit which can exhaust one in an endless effort to fulfil the need without ever truly satisfying oneself. This insane belief, partially fuelled by fear has caused people to manipulate, hurt, and devour others for their own good. Poverty is the cause of the most deaths in the world. You see, it has never been the lack of anything else that has caused this world to suffer so much. It is a mere lack of love.

Establishments have set in stone these beliefs, making slaves out of the common man, selling the goods that you are not *good enough* to buy. In essence, merely liking yourself is perceived as a great rebellious act. Achieving a superficial level of materialism – fame and fortune, a new car or house, or clawing your way to the top of the executive ladder only to be pushed into a hole in the ground a few years later is a false perception of success. Who cares about all these things, when you return to dust you won't own anything. The mansion and all your gold will be left for someone else. However, the experience of doing what you love in the service for others will be left as your legacy. Good and beauty, peace and joy, will live on, life is a continuation and not an ending. Michelangelo did not leave his enthralling heavenly art just for us to love, within his masterpieces he leaves a message for future generations to interpret.

Life is not about accumulation but about experiencing the fullness of life and that can only start to happen when you give attention to the purpose of your own life creating a reason to be here. We shouldn't wait, we might never realise the potential of our real self.

Nothing can substitute the good feeling that lies within when you create a daily sense of purpose. If you can do this you can then call yourself rich. Feeling good about yourself rarely has to do with surface reality but rather on internal acceptance and a daily sense of purpose. The world cannot give you confirmation for who you are, for this is only a reflection of yourself in the world through the metaphoric mirror of life. To think we are anything more than who we truly are – an amazing human being, is an illusion of grandeur. Thinking that owning that mansion will save you from death, or that your worldly riches can sooth away the pain of your insecurities, worries and fears, are a false prophecy.

I hear you saying it is all well and good being loved, but I've still got bills to pay, children to provide for, a home to run. Of course, life's peripherals are very important, the reality is we have bills that need to be paid, we have financial commitments, we need things to make our life more comfortable. However, you are stressed and tired of the merry-go-round of it all and deserve better – much better than just to exist. You are here to thrive not just to survive: in short, life's consumables may be nice but if you live for the craving of consumption, then, you will be consumed. If you live this way you will become a slave of your own creation. It takes brutal honesty within yourself, and there is no shame in admitting that we have been chasing the wrong tail in life. The irony and real truth is that you have the power that creates the wealth of abundance in your own life. This may offend you, especially if you have always struggled, but my concern is only that you realise the truth – that there is only one law: what you believe to be so can come to be true for you.

Every single person has something of value to contribute and express. The ability to achieve anything cannot be attributed to ownership of confidence, but rather in the ability to become confident in a new skill and endeavour. Love breeds that self-confidence required to attempt new things. To affiliate to all of life's creation is not about what we do to succeed but rather how we do it, the focus on your self will awaken self-motivation and natural skills and talents that have laid dormant inside. You become self-motivated through love. If you haven't got a job, then you are more likely to attract the right job when you feel you have something to give. Your outward self-expression is always connected to what you love and value most in life, and, consequently your profession is usually closely linked to who you are as a person.

Whatever you love doing, work towards it. There may be many sacrifices you need to make in order to get to doing what you love, but one thing it won't feel like is hard work. Of course, we can't always be doing what we love to do but we can always be working towards it. Many eureka moments have been realised when a person has become focused on their self-values and self-interests. A short cut to the mastery of a great life is to focus on your own life, your own business and affairs, this will bring your focus back to the integrity of self-love. If you're in a job and you

don't feel creativity or do not passionately adhere to it anymore, love will turn the abhorrence to something you enjoy and become more meaningful. As I've said in the spiritual practices I gave you earlier in the book, choose what excites you, follow your bliss even if it seems unreal at this moment. The more you follow your true desires the more you will get to achieve them – and quickly too.

I had a client who was creatively uninspired and dreaded going to work. She worked for a law firm and was very good at what she did, but I could see she had outgrown her position. I advised her to start loving her job and reminded her that once she had loved what she did... so the love was always there, but had been lost due to the complacency that generally happens when we stop growing and start dissolving into the background of fantasy and procrastination. She went to work and started blessing herself with love, she blessed her manager, her colleague's and her clients. After a short while she received a call from a law office that was helping her with a case she was working on. She asked after a certain gentleman who she knew worked there only to be told that he had died. Saddened by the news she talked of what a good man he was, and through the conversation she was told that they were in need of someone to fill the position. She couldn't think of a better law firm to work for and started her new job some weeks later.

Another client of mine was in a failing business. Through our conversation I noticed he was more interested in turning a profit than in giving a service – a very easy mind-set to get into. I suggested he started focusing on his client's needs instead of his own. We put a programme together and looked at areas in his business where he could give more. We both agreed that the business needed more love – from the premises through to the clients. So, we decided he would bless his clients individually as they entered the premises with an abundance of love. He blessed the phone with love, the building, anything connected with the business he blessed with love, and more importantly he started to love himself in the process. Within a short while his business became busier with new clients and old.

You will discover new ideas and inspirations to move on and grow when you spend more energy on working towards loving what you do even if you have fallen out of love in the short term. Instead of wasting vital energy on hating what you do and never doing anything about it, do what you have to do to get to where you need to go.

As soon as love is involved, joy is present, and that feeling of well-being, of connection with the divine-self becomes our true reality.

It doesn't matter what age you are, our purpose is the same – to feel love. To say our purpose is purely our vocation would mean when we retire our purpose is over, and for some that is what actually happens. You often hear when a person retires they meet an early death for they feel their purpose in life has ended. The best thing to do is to create a daily sense of purpose so that as you wake up every single day you know who you are and what you are here to do. This feeling is priceless. The meaning of life is to love, and grow that love in whatever you are doing. You are the purpose. You are the secret to a purposeful life.

Money, and your vocation in life are connected, it's the natural process of what we give we receive. There is a law that governs our outflow – work, labour, self-expression; and the inflow – salary, income, the fruits of your labour. Focus on what you wish to achieve and you will achieve it far quicker. The task in your hand is more important that the cash in your hand. Always expecting an instant reward for what we are doing turns your life into a means to an end instead of the means creating the self-fulfilment that it should do. As I write this book the enjoyment and sometimes fear that is present in me that nudges me to write and get my readers to understand the concept of love is my main focus. Other rewards if any, are secondary and should always be so.

Money itself is a means of exchange. There is no evil in money in spite of it being said that it is the root of all evil. Money itself has no power, only the person using it for their own needs. The elite use it to subconsciously define their power and self-worth. The rest *want* to define their self-worth and power with it. These are illusions caused by the teachings of the world. All of this is vanity and chasing after the wind. We have to go beyond the value of money and what it is worth to us and understand that in reality, love is all there is. If the basic function of money is to exchange, then the value behind it can only be of love. You think you are buying your favourite pair of shoes with money, you're not, love is behind the transaction: Love is the true buying power. I knew a client who always travelled to far away destinations. When I asked him how he could afford it on his modest salary he replied 'because I love traveling and I seem to always have the money to do it too.' He didn't know of course, but the love for travel created the opportunities for him to go traveling. You will always have in your life what you love. The law of creation cannot work in any other way.

There are so many myths surrounding money that it has turned the masses into its lovers, which in turn has both fuelled greed and created poverty. The money you have is not connected to its value but rather the value you think you are worth. If you believe any of these falsities that your net worth is more important than your self-worth, then it is likely that you will be in short supply of it for the rest of your life, as money comes from an expression of what you are giving, loving and being, this can only come from your self-worth and self-belief about yourself.

Your core beliefs concerning money effect how much money you have and will receive; the salary you have is the worth you have, not the job you do. It is always about the worth you have attached to yourself. I know many people who are in the same career who get paid considerably different salaries than each other. This has nothing to do with their jobs but their self-worth and their beliefs in abundance and the relationship they have with money. A belief in scarcity will breed a lack into your life. Until you realise the truth that you and you alone create the reality you live in, scarcity will be your only truth. These core beliefs are sometimes hard to detect and are promoted so frequently and personally through the media, governments and hierarchies to keep the mass controlled and subservient, that the person who realises they can create their reality is the luckiest person alive!

Our lives are abundant with ability to create. It isn't about stealing from the rich to feed the poor, it is about teaching everyone to believe in this abundance – it's about everyone winning. We never take from another when we are truly prosperous, we merely create more of what is already there. The universe is abundant with what already exists, and because the universe is within us we share that abundance. The kindest thing you can do for everyone is to take responsibility to create more of what is in the realms of you already. As I prosper I don't take from another, I create a belief for another that all you need exits in abundance and that there is plenty of it. We can never take from another what already exists in ourselves, nothing was ever created before it actually existed, it has to exist for us to create it. All the abundance that you wish for is already here, awaiting manifestation. If we don't believe this to be true our hidden beliefs of unworthiness, scarcity, and self-denial will always take precedence in our lives as we consciously change our mind so we will witness this truth for ourselves; merely acknowledging you are your own creator creates trust in yourself – and in abundance. There is a true saying: if you believe you can ... you are right, and if you believe you can't... you are also right.

There is an abundance, and your reality will change through the persistent use of all the *Spiritual Practices* I have invited you to participate in. Do this and you will prove you are a creator of abundance. Your purpose is to create to bring an abundance into this world; as I've said many times your purpose is to love creating for the love of it. As we love ourselves more each day we value ourselves more and this self-worth not only makes you feel better about yourself it increases the natural flow of abundance in your life. This is why I promote love to come first in any situation you have, from lack of money to lack of accommodation, lack of work, to lack of loving relationship. Love is always the cure to any negative mind-set.

Our mind-set around the beliefs of money is very poor. We feel bad for not having enough and guilty for having too much. I would like to invite you to use positive self-talk suggestions to balance the dual feeling of wanting money but also at the same time fearing it. These suggestions have been specifically designed to counteract the negative beliefs you have about money so you can realign back to a natural positive mind-set.

The Spiritual Practice 'Self-talk' may help with this.

A wise successful man once told me if you want more you've got to invoke the law of creation. He left me with a saying that I could never forget and it has helped me rebalance my beliefs concerning money; he told me:

'Invoke, and you'll never be broke'.

Here are a few suggestions, but always try to create your own to suit your own beliefs:

I am open and receptive to new opportunities that allow me to follow my passion that pays well.

I now attract the right job for me that pays well doing what I love to do.

My work is my play.

I deserve to do what I love to do.

My income is constantly increasing.

I deserve the best here and now.

I am infinitely surrounded by abundance.

I NOW attract Money easily, abundantly, infinitely, in wonderful ways

I am a money magnet

It feels good to have and enjoy money

Money comes to me easily and effortlessly

I save more money than I spend, and all my investments and savings are profitable.

It is safe for me to have money.

I bless the money I have.

It feels good to save money and let money work for me.

I am open and receptive to new avenues of income.

Having lots of money feels good.

MY income is constantly increasing.

I allow myself to create abundance for my life.

I am grateful for the abundance of money in my life.

Use these suggestions to invoke the law of creation daily for at least five minutes. Preferably in the morning as your mind is fresh and receptive. You will see in time you have the power and love to create your own reality. Trust in this process, life will give you the exact amount that you allow yourself to have. If this offends you then you are holding on to untold unworthiness that will keep you into a poor state of mind until you claim back your own worthiness. The abundant universe always responds to you. You can never get rich with a poor mind. Enrich your mind and your life will grow. Believe in yourself and invoke what you want, you will always get what you have asked for.

We will never understand true abundance until we harness this law of creation for ourselves and when we do we will experience the overwhelming feeling of knowing that the power to acquire abundance of any kind lies within us, be it money, loving relationships, self-expression, joy, peace ... whatever you wish for.

This is true prosperity.

CHAPTER 8: A RETURN TO LOVE IN ACCEPTANCE.

The kiss of life is the kiss of death – it ends all conflict, pain and disharmony in the person who has let go and decided to love life anyway.

Acceptance and surrender are the two wonderful qualities of love that can open up the spiritual dimension of the temple of love within you. When you surrender, pray, and accept, you are truly letting go of all that plagues you, and by surrendering to yourself to God the life force of love that is within you opens.

Whenever we intentionally surrender, we give way to something far bigger than the fear that is controlling our lives. Surrendering opens channels to deep reservoirs of creativity, intelligence, clarity, determination, wisdom, and choice. Fear cannot survive in you if when you accept its shadow of constant worries, you liberate yourself from its control and its illusionary demands of how life should be. By knowing fear, other than that which is instinctive and that has come into play when we are in physical danger, is to know that mostly what we experience is caused by the ego – a false sense of self that demands your life to be other than it actually is. Simply knowing that the mind's ideas, assumptions and opinions are the main cause of misery, and being aware of how our mind plays havoc with us when we try to rid ourselves of any of these preconceived ideas, is the quickest route to releasing worry and fear from your life.

When you are able to let go of your burdens you also release the strangle-hold you had on resisting them in your life.

What we resist we then persist with through the law of attraction.

When you love, accept, and surrender, every aspect of the fragmented insecure self becomes whole again. Something just happens when you let go. You allow something far greater, stronger, wiser, and calmer to guide your path to this infinite intelligence of love itself. You align yourself with the reality of that moment. We don't ever deal effectively with individual conceptual thoughts relating to a given situation, but we will always instinctively know what to do when we are actually facing a challenge that needs resolving. Dealing with whatever needs to be dealt with at the time it needs to be done is the only sane way to live. Reality happens not before, but as we are living our lives.

Whatever is or isn't happening in your life has an effect upon you: if it is good, then appreciate it. If it feels bad, then it is an experience, and as long as you learn, nothing is wasted. The gap between not knowing what to do, and knowing what to do is from where most of our life lessons are acquired. It's not necessary to master everything in order to make use of everything, challenges serve their purpose when we learn from them. As we grow, you will have no need for them anymore as you shall become what they have taught you.

You need to be very courageous to face your false self. The mask that underlines fear disguises itself, it is not true. Conceptual fear can be likened to a ghost; you know it's not real but it can still be quite a scary experience. It must be always accepted and never fought as you will learn that everything ends well if you let go and let love. If you simply allow change in your life to occur without opposition, acceptance becomes the torch you have chosen to hold. In those moments of darkness, when your attention embraces that thought of self-sabotage, hate, and raw unhappiness, by leaving behind your old self and letting go you leap into the unknown, and only then will you find out what you are truly capable of becoming. Focus on that gap between what you think you are and who you truly are with love, compassion, and kindness. If you do this, you will never need to look back or forward again.

It can be said fear is an illusion, so why does it feel so real? How can something that doesn't exist cause us so much pain? The answer is that you believe you are that subject or object you identify with. The person who breaks a relationship, has lost their job, or who is ill, becomes the reflection of what they are expressing. Humans have become accustomed to fear of change because they are creatures of habit, or at least their minds are. This is why love is the only antidote to fear, for it not only replaces fear but can turn it into something good and meaningful. The inevitability of all this is that life forms are to always evolve, nothing can stand still and say the same. Therefore, we either go with the positive flow of life and grow, or we resist it and crumble. Just be willing to know that whatever the result is, it is for the greater good. Don't be satisfied with simply knowing about the transformational tool called surrender, make it a commitment to use this daily within yourself.

Do not be a worrier; be a warrior. Live this life of ours as though you are going to love and accept like you have never done before. You need to break the illusion of fear and choose to turn away from it with your feet firmly on the ground. Have you noticed that life is chaotic? Life is always in the divine chaotic order of trust. Make the decision to either to accept or ignore it by choosing love again and again. Your every thought, word and action is a statement to the universe. This is what I do and it has become who I am.

The vision of replacing every fearful thought with a loving thought will improve your life dramatically. If you catch yourself feeding through negative thoughts, flip them over. Don't entertain any of them but replace them with loving thoughts of yourself. I love myself, and I am always loved and always safe.

Whatever you are missing in your life is always missing in you. If you don't own what's rightfully yours, then you miss what's rightfully yours. What is yours? Love, peace, and joy.

As you harness back the love into yourself, the process will become automatic and after a while, instant. Through love, your responses will always be truth, compassion, kindness, and integrity. True surrender makes you authentic, your divine light will shine through. When you are confronted with fear your responses will be the indication of how much love you have harnessed.

As *J. K. Rowling* said in *Harry Potter and the Goblet of Fire:*

> **'If you want to know what a man's like,
> take a good look at how he treats his inferiors, not his equals.'**

We will know within ourself that we have understood reality when our words, thoughts, and deeds are in total cohesion with one another.

When love is truly there you won't be able to hurt yourself or others anymore for the fear that causes hurt has gone. Love is the ultimate tool of respect, and respect for humanity is the reverence you hold for yourself. Humans are joined by two strengths: love and empathy. This is what makes us real. When you know the truth that fear doesn't really exist as a tangible emotion once you realise that love is the power, then this reality becomes you. You have reclaimed your forgotten self.

> ***Sometimes life offers no explanation...***
> ***... you have just got to trust it.***

CHAPTER 9: FINDING PEACE IN A RETURN TO LOVE

There are many aspects of love but one of the most crucial of all is peace. Peace is an underlying feeling of love that creates the sensation of tranquillity and serenity. When you are at peace, your journey becomes pleasant and joyful. There doesn't need to be an apparent reason, for this joy as peace comes without conditions. Many have found this inner peace at the most trying of times; in situations of total hopelessness when in a place of sheer grief people are still able to find a sense of peace. They seem to naturally be able let go. Anyone who suffers loss will generally feel this inner peace once the raw emotions of sadness and anger have had their say. It may take a while but we all realise fairly quickly that the situation cannot be reversed, and our automatic response is to instantly give way to the feeling of peace when it overwhelms us. (As it does in times of such grief.)

Peace of mind actually means we experience peace from our own mind. Remember, our mind can be our best friend or our worst enemy. It makes constant undermining demands of how things should or could be. Through feelings of regret, guilt, and shame this way of thinking breeds torture for its host (us). You are the host of your own insecurities for it is your own mind causing them.

Having a neutral approach towards certain situations is a balanced way to lead your life. Everything has a divine place and order in our lives, but do not confuse control with order. Control is the root fear for humans. We don't really fear change as much as we fear the loss of control:

Once you let go of control, you let go of fear. It is as simple as that.

One of the greatest problems we face in life, is that we want to be the controller. It is a liberating and humbling experience when you give up control and allow serenity and peace to emerge into any circumstance in which you find yourself. It is not what happens to us that counts it's how we respond to what happens that bring us to a place of peace or pain. What we have to learn is rarely chosen, but what we choose to learn from situations is the greatest lesson we can learn on this earth.

The reason the world is so restless and disharmonious is because it lacks peace, and the reason for this is because it lacks love. Most of our disturbances come through our lack of integrity in the relationships we have with others and this is due to the disturbances and lack of integrity we have within ourselves at our very core. We will always hurt others if we are the ones hurting even though this is nearly always unintentional. Likewise, if we can love ourselves we are more likely to love others too. As the old saying goes: *hurt people hurt others.*

If we forget to love ourselves, we forget to love others. Loving another is never enough if you can't love yourself, for you will always hold the belief someone outside of yourself is responsible for your peace and wellbeing. Instead of loving others for who they are you will be handing them the responsibility to take care of you which will cause them lack of peace. You are responsible for your own happiness. If you don't believe this you will be unhappy. Believing others are the cause of our lack of peace and disharmony within one's self is the main cause of misery for everyone concerned. The differences that divide us are judgments of each other. Let everyone be who they are, it's their journey not yours. Live and let live. Peace is simple: find peace within yourself and you will make peace with everyone else.

Failing to see that you are part of humanity is man's biggest downfall and causes him a lack of harmony. When we see ourselves as separate from everyone else we lose our sense of belonging to the whole of humanity. Once this connection with humanity is obscured, the alignment with serenity is obscured too. You see everything and everyone to be the problem and cause. In short, inner peace is realised through a shift in how you perceive your true self. By reclaiming your own life, you give yourself a lifeline to become whole again and connect with humanity.

To live a life completely lacking love is to live one of disharmony and suffering. A loving mind is worth more than all the riches in the world. Nothing can come close to the feeling of harmony, serenity, and peace within a feeling of unity. Mother Theresa perhaps said this best:

'If we have no peace, it is because we have forgotten that we belong to one another'

For this to take place, man must have a sense of self-awareness – a true knowing of who he really is. We can only recognise the same love within one another when we recognise the love within ourselves.

I believe true lasting happiness is possible, when we reclaim our everlasting peace. Peace is quintessentially who we are. This recognition takes a great deal of inner acceptance that starts with who we are, what we have done, and faith in who we will become.

We came in peace, and we shall leave in peace. What happens in-between is up to us.

What happens now is your choice: What does it matter if the bus is late or if it is a rainy day? What does it matter if your food is not to your liking in a restaurant? What does it matter what she or he said? What does all this pettiness really have to do with the reality of your true life? Do not allow anything outside of you to compromise your true sacred bond with peace. We live in an imperfect world because we choose to see an imperfect world. The choice has always been ours. Possibly until now you didn't realise you created what you have chosen to see.

If you are not at peace, it is usually a sign that you have to change something inside you, and that change always begins with acceptance. This isn't defeat but rather a way of allowing a higher perspectives of wisdom to enter our self-awareness. Love, truth and compassion will enter, aiding our understanding of all the situations that life throws us.

The miss-teachings of the world have truly caused our values, beliefs, and opinions to appear unrealistic and for us to be misled. In truth, it's not that the problems are the problem, it is that we have been conditioned to expect not to have problems . . . that's the problem! Sugar - coating life only delays the inevitable pain. We can gain by understanding the problems and using them to grow and become a wiser human being by applying this process of acceptance. Remember the proverb:

'A dose of adversity is often as needed as a dose of medicine'

We have been influenced, if not taught to merely seek pleasure in our environment and chase things for that purpose. We are told what happiness is, and how joy and peace can still be found in the material world. We are also sold on the idea that if you found your perfect life, (an illusionary concept to keep you from peace), you wouldn't need powerful institutions such as governments that appear to possess the truth to keep order within society. If you don't influence your own mind, society will control it for you. If they control what you think they will control what you create for yourself and who you become and more importantly your peace of mind.

Don't allow the search for perfect peace through pleasure and release to consume or distract you from your experience and growth in life. Accept that life is never going to be without challenges. The irony is that once you accept this, your life will improve and become easier to manage. It is crucial to be able to see any situation objectively by looking at the results that it yields. Only then can you make a proper judgment of what to do or not to do; the only truth that we need to know is the truth inside us. We came into this world from within, we will leave from within, so the only truth that is absolute is also from within. Make a proclamation of the truth that you now understand that you are the creator of your own experiences.

This is your life and it has been waiting for you to discover it. Up until now you may have been thinking that life is hard and is a struggle, and so by the law of attraction you have subconsciously and unintentionally created problems for yourself.

The process of life can so easily be misunderstood and its true purposes missed. If you don't believe you are the creator you will fall victim of your own circumstances, which will incarcerate you in unhappiness. This is the very reason we can't find harmony outside of ourselves. We can look, but will never find it. The only truth that can bring us back to a place of deep meaningful humanity is to realise our life is the most precious gift. Never will there be a time or space that will be you again. You are meant to thrive not merely survive. Yes, there is a magic answer for how to live the perfect life of depth and meaning; by merely consciously creating, your life will become based on the reality of the moment. For you to personalise this to true effect you are going to need to implement love, kindness and true compassion, only then can love bring you back to the place where all is one and one is all... where human life is realised, respected, and cherished.

Remember, you are in a relationship with everything, everyone and everywhere. Make your peace be known, and go beyond form and matter. Only then, will you experience peace of the soul that is far more valuable than words can ever describe.

The seasons will come and go, but love will always stay for it is the only thing that is real. Remember that anything real, does not change. Situations are temporary. Look back at your heartaches and failures and ask yourself honestly: where are there now?

To aid yourself back to peace and love, you must first acknowledge your lack of it. What message is it trying to teach you? What can you change, leave out, or accept? Listen to yourself because, there is no one else who knows you better. External signs will always show you the level of consciousness you are expressing. Be mindful and pay attention; take a moment to stop and notice what you're actually experiencing. Spend a few minutes merely observing your state of mind, not by judging thoughts, emotions, and fears, but by recognising your awareness of them. Observation is liberation: merely observing your emotions will dissipate them. You become the awareness that allows peace to be felt. You are the soul witnessing human emotion that allows you to be freed from your own negative mind-set.

This inner awareness is enough to bring you back to inner peace. To be aware, takes no effort, but the effects it can have on situations and circumstances are drastic. It is not necessary to know everything to make sense of everything, the understanding comes from a sense of awareness and a feeling a knowing. If you try too hard to know without first having an awareness of these things, you will bring stress and anxiety into every situation.

Have you ever noticed that when you tried to think of someone's name you couldn't remember? You may have been sure you knew the name, but then a few minutes later, when you have let go of that impulsive immediate desire to remember, the name appeared in your mind from what seemed like nowhere. Or, when you are waiting for that important call that doesn't come, but as soon as you have forgotten about the call the phone rings! This rule of process applies to any problem-solving or when you need to know anything. If your attention is obsessive i.e. thinking for answers, it blocks out your inner wisdom... and any new ideas, coming through from your inner core. Writers suffer from this problem, it's called writers block: As I was writing this book I would come across times where inspiration was not coming through, I would leave the paragraph and give my attention to other jobs. In that gap created by not overthinking, inspiration would flood through me. Your intellect is a very powerful and useful tool and the mind, when used properly can give us great insight when we simply let go and merely observe the situation.

Observe and let go

A lapse in peace is always a reminder for you to return to the sanctuary of love again. When you experience a state of anxiety and fear, ask yourself – is it a thought of what might happen or is it actually happening now? Anxiety derives simply from projecting your thoughts into the future and imagining something negative. Give the present your attention and these emotions won't have such a grip over you. As I've said previously, fear is an illusion which always relates to a future thought of what could, or might happen. The greatest danger facing us is ourselves – our irrational fear of the unknown.

We have the power to change our inner pain by realising we are the cause of it.

There's no such thing as the unknown. These are the things temporarily hidden from us, currently not understood. Focus on where you are at this very moment. This action stops you worrying about the future and shows you sense in what is happening now.

Love is our highest good. Recognise love as a force that is always protecting you. When change occurs in your life, you can be sure that things are turning for the better. The job you didn't get, the relationship that ended, the missed opportunities – they were all protection from this invisible force sheltering you from their false power and preparing you for highest good. This force of love is not unlike a parent protecting its child from harm, the parent will always take the sharp object away from the child for their own good. These sharp objects are like the toxic relationships that you couldn't let go of, but they will collapse before your very eyes. The obsessions of becoming more successful through material gain is a falsity. What happens if one day you were to get fired? You would then realise that if it hadn't happened, you probably wouldn't even be there at that point in time for all of the stress that pursuing illusionary necessary successes would have brought. Everything that doesn't happen is as important as those things that do, you are being prepared for something better which always is for your utmost good. Be thankful for closed doors, detours, and roadblocks, sometimes they protect you from paths and places not meant for you. In time, you will be able to look back at all the things that didn't happen in your life and realise you had a lucky escape. You are never alone; love is guarding you at all times.

'Be brave and remember love is your only defence and if you adopt the adage 'No fear no anger' nothing much can touch you'

Stuart Wild

Waiting for your situation to change is an anomaly because you are creating it in the first place by destructive thoughts of self-doubt, self-criticism, and self-hate. Every negative thought is a by-product of how we feel about ourselves. Your current reality is a result of your thinking. All of that will totally change as you begin to change your thoughts and feelings. Don't wallow in misery, let it go – surrender it, and as you give up the fight within yourself life simply becomes easier to manage.

Being negative only makes a hard journey more difficult.

All you need to know is that you are at peace at this moment? This very moment – not the next second of your life, this very moment – now as you are reading these words. If you are, which I'm sure you are, then peace will arise within you instantly because when we are intensely experiencing the present in this way we have no other time to worry.

Say, and feel the truth:

'I love and accept myself, and I am safe now.'

We live in an adverse world and through those adversities we can experience our true inner self. This is a call for internal/spiritual awakening; a revolution in your life, perhaps a call to dedicate yourself to help others. You are invited to change and become an instrument of help for others to play by being the advocate of peace. If you never experience a lack of peace through life's challenges, you won't recognise this reconciliation of love and peace and the serenity that lies beyond.

A heart that has experienced a lack of peace due to adversity, is a heart that becomes pure. Forgiveness, compassion, humbleness, and kindness, are challenges of hardship that make you more real, more authentic and empathetic as a person. The meek are not weak for they are strong enough to love, and love is the most powerful force in the universe. When we think with love life becomes powerful, when we think without love life becomes dreadful.

Humans are joined by two strengths: Love and empathy. The empathy you have for others is the divine grace that knows one's pain, but nevertheless at the same time knows nothing that is not real can hurt us. All human pain and suffering is temporary, for nothing real outside ourselves exist. The mere reflections of ourselves and experiences can always be changed through being self-aware.

Without awareness, nothing would exist for you. Ask yourself, what would your daily experience be without awareness? There would be no content to the book of life if one wasn't conscious. This consciousness is who we truly are, we are the observer of the observed. Although every choice of thought, word, and deed, makes things seem either more peaceful or more difficult, this experience is interchangeable on the basis of knowing you are the creator of life itself. A person who is connected with themselves in truth, love and acceptance, will deal with temporary situations from places of the eternal strength brought by peace from within themselves. They will know that true harmony is obtained through their peace of mind which always comes from their state of offering no resistance to what is. As we accept what is, we become more powerful than what is happening; we become wiser and see every situation more clearly. Something magical happens when you let go, you create a space to enable better things to enter your life.

The Spiritual Practice: 'Be thankful' will help you understand this.

Peace and love are inseparable, the more you love the more peaceful you will become. We are like the ocean: undisturbed by the changing of the tides when love is on our side. Everyone is looking for peace but if they do not find it within themselves they'll never find it anywhere else. Be more interested in what's happing inside of you than what surrounds you for what surrounds you was once inside of you. Thoughts of guilt, regret, resentment, grievances and sadness have brought you to a place of interest. Your lack of peace is a lack of understanding of this simple truth that causes so much pain, you are not at the mercy of the effect of your circumstances… you are the cause of them. If you feel bad about yourself, you are not being true to yourself. Sorry once again if this offends you, but the fact is when you feel bad you are having negative thoughts about yourself. It may be the case that your situation has brought about your lack of peace, but on further investigation you will see you are the one who creates what you feel.

There are two things you must remember: feeling bad of yourself is never true of yourself, and feeling good is the experience of truth. When we feel bad we turn down every opportunity of feeling loved, creative, powerful, joyous and peaceful. Making the choice to believe in the scarcity of our true existence is the cause of feeling not good enough. If thoughts could materialise instantly in our lives, we would be less inclined to cause ourselves to suffer. If a brick fell on your head every time you had a negative thought, you would be sure to stop thinking that way. Be focused on what you wish to experience, if we don't catch our negative thoughts they will turn into negative feelings, if we don't catch our negative feelings the will develop into negative circumstances or a poor physical state of being. Ask yourself these two crucial questions:

What do I want? And why aren't I allowing myself to experience what I want?

If we are honest with ourselves the answer to those questions is, we are easily distracted by our circumstance. Forgive yourself for making mistakes and remember, they are part of the learning curve. Everything has a purpose of showing you what you don't want to be, and in doing so, gives us the chance to choose again. Your lack of serenity is a wakeup call from your higher-self to focus on what you wish to experience for yourself. Make the commitment to yourself without judgment to become really self-aware of your state of being; ask yourself, are these thoughts positive or negative do they make me feel good or bad about myself?

Revisit the first *Spiritual Practice: 'Choice is a simple decision'* and *'Never judge yourself'* to help you with finding peace in a return to love.

Thoughts that bring about good feelings mean you are on the right track, and the ones that bring about bad feelings mean you are not.

The key to inner peace is to go within and accept what is. Circumstances change. The strongest species are the ones who are responsive to changing themselves. The world says; once you find peace everything will fall into place. Closer to the truth is choosing to love and accept your life - this is the only place where you can consciously change reality and thus find your inner peace.

CHAPTER 10: A RETURN TO LOVE IN HAPPINESS.

Love does not depend on happiness, but happiness depends on love. Unhappiness has become a normality in modern day society. Humans are less happy now than a hundred years ago where it can be said the world did not flourish with material gain and luxury. The pursuit of happiness has been the quest for many, especially in a system that has lost its sense of community and kindred spirit. On an individual and collective level, we have lost the most important commodity of allowing integrity and unity to drive our society forward in harmony and love. In believing we are separate from one another we lose the ability to be compassionate, kind, and humble. These qualities are one of the main ingredients in a contented self-fulfilling life. The deficiency of being unable to demonstrate love is of course due to the forgotten self not knowing who we truly are.

Think of a time when you really felt harmonious.

By analysing this you will find that the answer lies in our human connections. Material things can't truly make you happy for they are inanimate objects. Humans need each other for true happiness. Joy emanates from each of us, and that inner joy is felt when we are able to express love, kindness, and compassion.

When we are self-fulfilled with a purpose that includes the giving of love, joy, and creativity to others, we will find true contentment. The fastest route to inner joy is when you have chosen to raise your core inner values. Until we remember our true unique sense of self and discard the illusion of fear, we will be continuously in pursuit of happiness. We will merely remain comfortable with being uncomfortable.

Negative emotions have made us quite narcissistic in our societal behaviours, seemingly we enjoy the pain and drama that they inflict on ourselves and others.

> **'Your worst enemy cannot harm you as much as your own unguarded thoughts'**

Buddha

This narcissistic behaviour is covering the true identity and sacredness of the forgotten soul. It does not matter about your background or class of societal structure from which you emerge. People in general have become less content. In fact, some of the most dysfunctional people are the very rich and famous, displaying actions of pure insanity and self-deception. Obviously, we can see that this way of existing is a very dangerous way to live. The human race has become very unhappy and discontentment is rife in most modern civilisations. If humans are to evolve, they must reclaim the true nature of self-fulfilment to experience purpose, joy, love, and the true serenity of unity again.

> **We must live and learn that life is always an inside job.**

Constantly looking to acquire more and more by way of material things does not and will not bring you happiness. A contented person is one who has found their purpose and their truth of who they are, and lives and shares that truth. It is someone who rejoices within and who finds self-satisfaction and thus is able to then give themselves entirely. You have the capacity to have a wealth of joy, love and harmony, but that always starts and ends with you. I believe happiness is not a total certainty that happens every day when we allow it to become conditional, but the inner peace and joy within you can make the difference. When your happiness is conditioned by external circumstances, remember that inner peace can be achieved by merely accepting and loving yourself... which is always unconditional.

As you begin to intentionally focus your life through self-preservation, self-honour, love and acceptance, you will start to see changes; indirectly through your feelings, but more directly through your day to day life. The force of love will start a shift to change things, maybe little things at first, but these will start to move your outer realities to reflect your inner reality.

As you raise your vibratory frequency of love, your life will accelerate. It may seem at first that things get worse before they get better but of course this is not the case, all you are experiencing is a shift from negativity to positivity. Love works in mysterious ways. Whatever changes you do or do not make, allow love to take its course. You may not change what you do, but merely how you are doing it. This means you will simply and quite naturally remain in the same place but feel very different indeed about your life.

For love to really work through us we need to have faith in the face of change. As we consciously love and accept ourselves you will find outdated thinking patterns that may have been stuck within you for years will be changed. Love will change anything unlike itself back to itself. It will enter every area of your life's reality, tipping over and throwing out the old and entering the new. The underlining problems, the difficulties with your relationships, your finances, your health, will all face a reality check. Remember, love doesn't change the circumstances but it changes *you*, and by doing this, it is impossible for your outer world to remain the same as your inner world has changed. It becomes like the changing of the seasons from summer into autumn – the leaves may change colour but they are even more beautiful when they have fallen.

As we love, we become stronger, wiser, and more transparent to the truths within us.

It may feel really uncomfortable to see the changes in your outer world, but by standing still in that moment of confusion and lack of understanding you will see the truth that precedes it. It is natural to feel unease as these things change. Remember you are rebuilding a new life after saying goodbye to some of the illusionary ideas you previously took comfort in. The main reasons humans haven't evolved spiritually and in fact seem to have stopped in this area of evolutionary growth, is because we've been in the fearful shadows for so long. It can be too painful to become warmed by the light of love again. It is sometimes very hard to believe that humans have become accepting of a really unacceptable way of living.

As *Frederic Nietzsche* said:

'Sometimes people don't want to hear the truth because they don't want their illusion destroyed...'

It is your emotions experienced in the past, and fears of the future that have caused your imprisonment and unhappiness which you yourself bear witness too. Past emotions are no more than a habitual thinking pattern that can make your life senseless. Witnessing these emotions without judgment or self-criticism is the key that will help you dramatically. Being aware of your negative emotions can free you from them, for only when we are aware can we make positive changes in our lives. Imagine sitting in the cinema watching a horror film. Your senses will be stirred, but you know you are not part of the drama; you are only the one that is observing. This is exactly what happens when we bear witness to our own emotions – we become very self-aware of the varying degrees of emotion within us, but they need not all be part of us. This detachment can occur when we have the ability to merely continue with our life without allowing emotions to play their part, therefore without judging a single thing. You will see that the action required for this ability is to merely observe your emotions so that they won't become so personal. Negative emotions disable you from taking the appropriate action. These emotions will cause you to become constantly indecisive.

Do you find yourself being constantly indecisive? Even with simple tasks stress plays a major role in indecisiveness. Fears and anxieties about making the wrong decisions keep you incarcerated in situations and circumstances that are probably not good for you. A lack of self-confidence feeds indecisiveness. This indecision is a common notion to those who lack self-esteem, and among those who lack this, are a few people who find it hard to love and accept themselves. Feeling incapable makes you rely on others rather than doing what is important for yourself. You need to remember that the only bad decision is to be indecisive, because it leads to inactivity. Without action, there is no progress.

When love is in motion your fears, beliefs, and rituals will be replaced with new energies fuelling self-esteem and worth. Trust whatever love throws up. Emotions of fear, resentment, anger, and all that can lead to unhappiness, are there to be healed not buried. We are all wounded one way or another due to the miss-teachings of the world that lead us to believe that we are not good enough. Remember, the wounded make the best healers for they have accepted themselves for who they are and then made the changes required and many have then gone on to heal the pain in others. You owe one thing to yourself and that is to be authentic and honest about your own emotions.

Ownership of your life is self-empowering. On no occasion make an enemy of your situation as life has brought it to light for nothing can grow in the dark. Love changes everything created by fear.

Albert Einstein once said that you can't change your current situation with the same level of consciousness that caused it.

To say love is attached to a positive outcome rather than a negative result, is not quite right. We have all experienced negativity in one way or another, and while it is branded negative it will stay negative. The response to particular situations can be said to be either negative or positive in the eyes of the world. If we look closer, we see that our reactions towards any given event are the reflection of the happiness or disharmony from that moment in time.

Positivity and negativity are so interwoven in the tapestry of our life that one can't survive without the other. A positive or negative outcome is down to an interpretation of the conceptual thought that creates the emotion. These interpretations always imply a limited perspective that derives from the false sense of self-ego. We may feel that what is happening shouldn't be happening, or we may ask ourselves why isn't something happening.

Acceptance is the voice of reason and wisdom that will guide you to freedom from the incarceration of your mind that tells you life has to be a certain way.

I once read a story of a wise man who won an expensive car in a lottery. His family and friends were very happy for him and came to celebrate.

'Isn't it great' they said. 'You are so lucky.'

The man smiled and said,

'Maybe.'

For a few weeks, he enjoyed driving the car. Then one day a drunken driver crashed into his car at an intersection and he ended up in hospital with multiple injuries. His family and friends came to see him, saying that it was really unfortunate. Again, the man smiled and said,

'Maybe.'

While he was in hospital, one night there was a landslide and his house fell into the sea. Again his family and friends came the next day and said,

'Weren't you lucky to have to have been in hospital.' Again, he replied:

'Maybe...'

This story shows that where there is no judgment there is an alignment with a higher order. Seemingly random events never exist in isolation. We can't control what we don't understand but we can make sense of things in our life when we merely allow life's happenings to be. In short, your judgment of life creates your judgment of self through circumstance. As we label things as difficult in our lives, we create feelings that actually make us feel worse. This is why one of the main spiritual practices I have invited you to participate in is that of being non-judgmental. As we move through our daily lives in a non-judgmental way we free the space within us for love to enter every situation or circumstance we may be going through. When love is involved you will be sure that only good will come out of any situation. If we criticise, we become negative and will fail to understand the benefits that are waiting for us on the other side of any difficult situation.

Love has no dualities. There is only one joy, one peace, and one love for us to feel the true inner joy that we need to adapt and change. Our attitude makes an enormous difference in our lives – pessimism is a sure way to keep yourself miserable.

Vow to adopt a new dominant positive mental attitude.

All this being said, you must remember not to allow positive thinking to merely become a substitute for positive action, it will only turn into wishful thinking. The law of attraction works with the implementation of consistent real action. Otherwise it would become just a device for satisfying purposelessness. Don't just wish for it to happen, anything worth having is worth working for. Be positive, act positive and you will manifest a positive reality for yourself.

When we take action within, and discipline ourselves to see only our preferences, good things happen. One thing that you do have in life is a choice to think for yourself. This unique opportunity is so over-looked and causes us grave consequence. In general, if we feel bad, then we have chosen to feel bad. This is a hard pill to swallow, but as we do so we will feel so much better and more empowered.

I would like to invite you to an instant three-way process which will take you from feeling bad to feeling good:

Step 1: Become aware and understand that you have generated these emotions somehow. You don't have to go too deep into this, but know that somehow you created what you are presently feeling, then just accept those feelings for one moment with the knowledge that they are for a purpose.

Step 2: Stop yourself from thinking those same thoughts. Investigate where you have fallen out of alignment with your higher self. You feel bad because you have lost sight of your true being. So get a clear perspective of what made you feel bad in the first place. Always start from the position of the way your mind thinks in order to change the way you feel.

Step 3: Ask yourself Who am I? And, what do I want to feel. This will reconnect your conscious vision to who you truly are and to who you truly want to become.

This book is about feeling the good and rising above the madness of this world. The more we feel good about ourselves the more the law of attraction works in our favour. When we feel good about ourselves the nonsense around us disappears and good opportunities arise. I don't believe in luck, but feeling good about yourself through changing how you think will give you the feeling of being the luckiest person alive. But all this requires action. It takes discipline through a daily conscious effort. There is nothing else to stop you achieving anything in your life – only yourself.

Feel the fear and do it anyway, that is the only true way to go with the flow of life.

There have been many great men and women that have faced the most adverse challenges which could at the time have been described as negative. Some were. Overcoming challenges brought them successes they had have never imagined.

Challenges are not supposed to paralyse you; they are supposed to help you discover who you are.

The mistakes we make are merely teaching us to remember that there is another choice; one that ensures our journey will always involve love. We grow through our errors, our weaknesses and vulnerability become our strengths. Your adversities become your victories, and you will have grown in strength, kindness, humility, and compassion. These are all the ingredients of a successful being.

Your personal development at any given time will determine the level of happiness you feel within your life.

Life wasn't meant to be simply tolerated and continuously challenging. The return to love will bring a balance into your life in a way that happiness can be felt. This is not for special occasions, but for making the daily occasions special. Love will make you content as it will draw happiness to you in ways that you would never have imagined. Love is light energy, which cleans the dense and heavy emotions in the body. This allows you to shine through.

The world is not your responsibility, but you do have a responsibility in the world; to care, to love, and to accept yourself and others.

As a love-maker, check in daily and reflect on what makes you happy. Ask yourself:

Who am I?

What would make me content?

What would I like to do, see, and become?

The very act of asking these questions invokes the soul to find that joy!

So often, we get caught up in simply being a parent, a spouse, a friend, and our happiness is put on the back burner. We have been taught to put the highest good of others before ourselves. This statement contains the essence of the trust; for what we do for others will be done to us. We are all one body, one love.

We have our own individual journeys that are ours to discover. This is not a selfish act but in fact a selfless one. When you prioritise your needs, the needs of others will also be met. As you become more self-content you will breed joy for others. It is that simple.

Take a good look at yourself now.

Be conscious as you contemplate your life. Become self-aware of a presence in you that is more than your mortal mind. Feel the clouded judgment of your personality disappear, leaving only love's intelligence to witness itself. Feel those sensations throughout your entire body. Try to look at your whole life from inside out. Review your current situation at least once a day as if you were listening to your friend's life story. We can always see other people's lives much more clearly than our own because we see things from another perspective. This is exactly the space we need to provide ourselves with. Daily self-contemplation will provide so much clarity in every area of your life.

Applying the *Spiritual Practice: 'Be thankful'* will help to ground your daily routine for a return to love in happiness.

The eyes of the soul will appear through the grace of your stillness as you contemplate your life, observing everything and everywhere. This is unlike day-dreaming, because you will become so aware of the life force within you.

Sometimes this action will spontaneously happen and you will not have noticed this before. However, what originally caught your attention was your soul wanting you to stop, look, and listen to aid you in your journey through life.

> **Stop, look, and listen to your life. 'If you change the way you look at things, the things you look at will change.'**

Dr Wayne Dyer

Life has become a decision-making process. Humans are bombarded with hundreds of decisions needing to be made on a daily basis. This compromises a peaceful existence, as a simple thing like just going out for lunch can become an ordeal with so many choices to be made.

Our societal systems are serious and rigid; they don't allow much space or time for you to decide what's best for you at any given moment. More often than not, we come to rely on others for answers. Although this can be helpful, all the answers you will ever need to know come from that place inside of you. If you first ask yourself these questions, then you will find that problem-solving and negotiating of any sort becomes easier and less frustrating to deal with.

> **'If you look for the truth outside yourself, it gets farther and farther away.'**

Tung Shan

All I need to know is revealed to me. I never make a decision without consulting myself first. I ask myself questions, and myself answers me back every time through the so-called serendipity of life. This state of vastness and divine intelligence within you appears out of nowhere, whenever we simply ask it for ourselves through quiet contemplation. Every answer you need for yourself, your family, and your friends should be asked in this space of contemplation. Love will help you on your journey as all you need to do is ask. When you have received that divine advice, or help in any situation, don't forget to thank yourself.

Here are some thought-provoking questions:

If I ask myself what is the main reason of why I am not happy? Is it the cause or the effect? Am I thinking more about what I don't want, rather than what I do want?

Most people feel they are somehow missing out in life. They are constantly thinking about want they don't want. Be a witness to your thoughts and words and you will find that most of your discontentment derives from a place within you that hasn't been capable of merely loving, accepting, appreciating, and respecting yourself.

Your life wasn't meant to be a struggle, and if you are constantly experiencing it as such then you have fundamentally forgotten that your true nature is a harmonious undulating flow of the moment by moment process of discovery. Your life doesn't need to be perfect for you to be perfectly joyous. You have got to be committed to being happy for that can only be experienced by you. You are the only one responsible for your happiness. If you don't believe this, you will remain unhappy. Happiness does not depend on where you came from or what you have – it depends solely on what you think. If not now, when will you become happy about yourself? Happiness comes from the heart not from your successes. Success is not the key to happiness but rather happiness is the key to every successful life. What do I mean by having a successful life? Simply, being happy.

CHAPTER 11: A RETURN TO LOVE IN DEATH

There is a sacredness and mystery towards death that has been denied, hidden and misunderstood. Culturally we believe that the body is a costume which you have borrowed for a while to experience life; that is, your experience of being yourself. Life happens. If we do not understand death, then we will never understand life; the two are automatically connected. To have one you must know and understand the other.

Life gives birth, death takes it forward; the beginning and the end are one – they are part of the eternal ring of life. You may have heard the saying 'the circle of life', this comes from the Disney film *The Lion King*. This simplistic childhood film expresses the meaning very effectively; being there for one another through hope and despair, love and hate and all difficulties, and that our lives are a chain of events that perpetuate a never-ending cycle of life. Love is forever expanding, evolving, and multiplying itself whilst we respond to nature.

This essence of love plays on a very important aspect of the *Spiritual Practice: 'Love yourself'*. This expenditure of love revolves around others and yourself, so in order to fully experience the circle of life so to speak, you must embody the notion of loving yourself as well as others.

The life form you have become accustomed to is a space for the soul to evolve and give it purpose to move on to the next dimensional experience.

The composition of the human body is made up of six elements; oxygen, carbon, hydrogen, nitrogen, calcium, and potassium. This composition is found in nature itself – we are the clouds, the sun, the moon, the ocean. We are no more than the fire that continuously burns, the water that flows around us, and the very air we breathe.

We are all going to die but when, where, and how is irrelevant. This holds true to the *Spiritual Practice* of *'Self-talk'* – you must make sure that it is never negative. Yes, we will all die someday, but focus not on this time but on the present. Concentrate on the good and not the bad. Leaving this life without getting to experience our true self as humans is bad in every sense of the word. Not knowing our true sacredness is the fear that holds us away from the sublime love we are. This shortcut in complacency leaves many having regrets of the life they could have led.

In general, if you are fortunate to experience a life of longevity, you will have experienced life flowing by. The truth of the matter is not that life flies by too quickly, but rather we are busy worrying about more important thing, one of them being to make your life perfect before you start living perfectly. Time itself is an illusion that is felt by age of events, linear mile stones, places and things we have identified with; the past has gone but the future holds no promises.

We still believe in time. The phrase should not be *'time is precious'*, but *'you are precious in time'*. If anything, the illusion of time can teach us that you will never experience this day again. The reality is time is precious – if you do not embrace your friends, family, animals, and natures beauty, in this moment of time, all sense of preciousness will be lost.

The closer you move towards self-awareness, the closer you will get to feel this reality that emerged through the life forms, before the action of birth and death. These are both involuntary actions out of our control. Finding reason for death is something that stops you living, and by questioning the unquestionable, your reasoning mind will spread fear throughout your life. As we have said, the fear of living is a false sense caused by the response of your ego, which is constantly trying to protect itself from the threat of failing, losing, and inevitably dying. Its fight to hold on to your last breath will be felt throughout your life, as feelings of anxiety, stress, and depression, all hold you back from living. Unless you accept birth and death as the continuity of life itself you will be under the illusion that the world is just your alpha and omega – your beginning and your end. Life is a wonderful comparing circle of sharing the end and the beginning of the eternal ring that can never be broken.

When the time comes for us to vacate, taking our next quantum leap, we will disappear back to the unknown from the place we came from. To say that we didn't exist before the transition to birth, would be like saying we won't exist after death. An entrance must exist for us to enter into the beginning of our life.

At best, we can see death as a doorway that connects us beyond the concepts into the unknown, where we will reside in peace until the next time to re-enter the flesh of man. This is one thing we will never know until we experience this sublime journey into the abyss for ourselves.

You are the life force, the substance that gives life its actual existences, as opposed to an idealistic or notional idea that you merely have a life.

The illusion of the mind that separates us from the love of ourselves and love of others, leaves no questioning when you witness the meaning and strength of the truth that lies within you. The foundations of our life, although externally cannot be seen, is what gives us strength and holds us up. So will our cognisance be stable when it has a strong spiritual foundation? We are connected to something that is immortal. Our real home is where there is love, peace, and a humility. Home really is where the heart is.

Think back to the *Spiritual Practice – 'Be thankful'*. Be thankful for life as you know it: if you have a home and family to love, be thankful. Do not dwell on what is missing, or you will be miserable until your death. Dwell on the present and be thankful for it.

As I became more self-aware of my true life, I realised love was the only and the essential truth. The more I loved, the more I had an interconnectedness with the unseen life force within me and within others. By connecting to the absolute truth you will sense an indestructible power from which you can never be separated –

this power is you. The recognition of love within ourselves is the coming together of love, not the parting.

The belief surrounding death originated from the dissociation with our true self, the divine and sacred soul. This dissociation caused us to make judgments to replace who we truly are, thus seeking ourselves outside the reality of life itself. Humans fear death because they believe the world is their home, and their complete truth. The attachment to the world causes the fear that we are mere mortals subjected to our death sentence.

The nature of the world is birth, old age, and ultimately, death; essentially the world is not real for everything is always changing. At best we can change the furniture around us to make our lives look prettier, but ultimately things are out of our control.

I remember feeling overwhelmed when first realising that I am eternal life, and that my body was no different from the car I drove to work every day. This self-realisation was my insurance that my father, and my loved ones who went before me, are very much still alive.

The life force that we live and breathe is the truth, and nothing but the truth, it shall defy the test of time.

Grief is a process of total desolation, anger, and sadness. This process takes time to heal. The gap between you and peace is the time it takes for you to accept the seemingly unacceptable. As human beings, through love and surrender we need to witness and forgive the illusion of death to know it has no value over us.

When the inevitable happens, all talk of surrender at first seems inconceivable. For most, accepting loss is the hardest things to bear, but there is no peace within you without acceptance. So how do we accept the unacceptable? We do so, by understanding that we can't force acceptance... and this state brings us through the portal to experience true inner peace. Acceptance is the greatest act of loving yourself for it will release you from the ever-decreasing circles that recycle the fear in your mind.

Give yourself time, speed, and space, to grieve. The *Spiritual Practice* of *'Solitude'* can help with this. Take yourself away from everyday life whilst you heal. Often, people will deny their emotions and bury themselves in further problems of transferred pain and denial, which inevitably they will have to face further down the line. Remember emotions should never be reasoned with but merely accepted for what they are – human emotions. These emotions are best challenged in a moment of solitude as only then can you experience everything at your core. No matter how hard it may be, taking these practices into account will make life easier to deal with.

Remember, we are never completely alone. We were not meant to take this journey of self-discovery by ourselves. Humans use words and labels to justify and ignore things they need to face and deal with. At times of sorrow, be witness to one another that true kindness, compassion, and sympathy is the proof that love never dies. For the ones who are left behind time will become the testament that love concurs.

Through grief you will experience that what we loved is not lost.

What we have loved becomes a part of us forever.

Trust in yourself, love God and the universe. Trust that you are connected to the trust within you that is your home. Remember:

'Where there is love there is life'

Mahatma Gandhi

Consider all these things when you are faced with the prospect of love and death. Remember the circle of life, remember to be thankful and love yourself. Remember *Solitude* as a *Spiritual Practice* to help you, but remember above all – you are not alone.

CHAPTER 12: A RETURN TO LOVE: THE BEGINNING OF AN END

The last leg of our journey is to understand that when you are ready and able to put into practice all the parts of the jigsaw, it puts an end to anything that might interfere with you being your true complete self. There will be no more suffering caused by your delusions of life because you will be able to let go of them. There will be no more constantly seeking for better without knowing what it is. No more blaming, justifying, or the manipulation and control of circumstances that we all inadvertently try to enforce from time to time whether we mean to or not.

When we meet this head on and put into practice the things we have talked about, we will have gained a true understanding of love and its affect upon the world. We become fully ready for a true return to love. This is the beginning of an end – not the end of our physical lives, but of our tarnished soul, and of our false sense of a spirituality that may have taken us down a different path up until now.

As humans we have always needed a sense of divine belief, it is inbuilt in our genetic make-up. This sense of need has been essential to our evolution and is engrained deep within us. For these beliefs to ever have grown and developed, love must have prevailed. Whether we place our faith in God, the universe, or just in ourselves, we must understand that the creator is within us. You are not only the body through which God, the creator, or physical science has allowed your soul to experience, you are the mind – the power, the source of divine creation within yourself. The mind is producing a universe of activity of one's own thoughts. You are this mind – the epic thinking centre, and what you think governs your life. This is so simple to understand and so easy to use that we might often wonder why we have been so long finding this out. The greatest of all truths is that man is just what he thinks himself to be; we will attract to ourselves what we think most about. We can only begin to govern our own journey when we take this complete control over our thoughts. Then, we can truly say this is the beginning of an end.

Even if you don't believe in a God, believe in yourself. You must believe you can by thinking you can. Think back to each day you wish to be returned, use the power of your imagination to create positive change in your life and eliminate the negatives. Give thanks to the spirit of life within you and love yourself every step of the way; these are steps that when followed will bring proof unto their own. Remember the seed that falls into the ground shall bear fruit of its own kind;

This is the law of creation.

We have also called it the law of attraction up until now, but to experience the sublime, to reach out to that beautiful place where we can all be if we truly believe, we have to become the creators of our own universe. This does not in any way negate from a belief of faith we have in a supreme being or an ultimate creator, more so it defines our own beliefs in such.

I am always working within the law of creation; this is a personal experience. You can never put yourself in exactly the same place as other people, no matter how hard you try. Although you may feel as one with them on a level of love, you are still unique and special. Each one of us has our own identity, our own thoughts and purposes. Each person you know has their own background, personality, and of course, point of view. Although you can always influence, you cannot change other people... and you shouldn't, this is something they must do for themselves. This may sound selfish to those not understanding how the law of creation works or to those who do not realise that the only person you can do anything about is yourself, but your concern should be for yourself. Being able to show that loving is a completely unselfish act leads to the action of giving of yourself. Your only concern is to be aware of who and what you really are, all you will then have to do is give yourself in love. Find the peace in you so you can give peace, find the love in you so you can give love, and find the joy in you so you can give joyously. The world doesn't need more successful people it needs more loving people.

You are here to represent love and participate, becoming part of its grand design. For that to take place we must realise we need to love each other. Like the universe needs you to experience itself, you need others around you to experience your true self. Not only do we need each other, we are each other, and through demonstrating love, we know it's our love to tear and share.

**Love is the language of the soul of the universe,
and all that lies within it.**

Our purpose is to end the illusion of fear and separation – you, me, them and us. The vision that we are but beautiful, magnificent, and multi-dimensional beings, that have the power to create wonderful things, is finally realised and awoken through this process of returning to love.

The more you love yourself the more you realise your true nature is to love. Your ability to generate feelings of love is unlimited, for love is an infinite creation. You can never stop creating more because you are part of it. When you love you are in complete and utter harmony with the universal autonomous process of creation.

Knowing love and experiencing love are worlds apart. Bring your worlds together by merely loving them. Don't wait for your life to be perfect before you start. Life is the mere process of living, loving, and learning together. Your mind will always rationalise and reason by telling you to start the process when things seem perfectly right. You might have thought when someone doesn't show me love I will hold mine in reserve too. Don't listen to this... love now.

There are no perfect conditions to demonstrate love in your life. Without action, you will never experience or witness any re-action of love's true purpose – to love one another. We can see that the *giver* of love is also the *receiver* of love.

The most important thing in life is to learn how to give love without instant gratification.

As we become more self-aware through the process of this return to love, we actually move closer towards our true reality. Our values will reflect the purpose, vision, and self-realisation, which will bring with it a sense of belonging and responsibility. We came here to fulfil life's true purpose of giving love. Yes. We came here to give of ourselves. If you were waiting for a more meaningful purpose, then you haven't grasped the meaning of life that we have been talking about. Love is the great multiplier. Only by multiplying can it fulfil itself, and by that, I mean fulfilling yourself. There is more joy in giving. Why?

Only in what we give to ourselves primarily and then to others can the law of creation work in multiplication. The laws that govern it only work in accordance to this principle.

When you have harnessed enough love from within yourself, (and you will know when you have), then your internal reality will reflect your external reality through its abundance of love, joy, peace, clarity, and wisdom. Only then can it be said that love is ready to fulfil its true purpose.

This vital turning point is where love is intentionally directed out into the world. You will need to give love back and show the world the truth – nothing but the truth. At this stage of the process, a true return to love will manifest itself through a natural, spontaneous, and gratifying act.

We can show our love by how we respect others; how we serve and how we honour each other. One of our greatest primeval needs is to create a very deep form of real unity between our souls. These are the greatest strengths on this earth. Unity is one of the highest principle laws of the universe; in fact, the universe's pure existence is within the law of interdependence. Your body could not have been created outside of the unified cells and atoms that make it. Music could not be created without first there existing the sounds made by every single thing that ever existed. Everything has a connection with each other.

We have been led to believe that we are mere fragments. These ideas, opinions, comparisons, and diversities, cause separation and dis-unity between us. This is the ignorance that society breeds; *if I give myself away, there will be less of myself.*

Look closer at your brothers and sisters; are they not like you? Do they not cry? Do they not bleed, or feel no pain? Are we not all identical in that we are all trying to figure out what the hell we are doing here? The compassion, kindness, and love you express shall be the compassion, love, and kindness you shall receive.

Unity is strength

A true act of love is shown in its unity. It is upon this fact that your very existence is built. It is this that is the foundation of every chapter in this book: No, you cannot know this intellectually, you cannot debate it, or substantiate it, you can only feel it and be aware of it as you express it through the fullness of loving for the love of it.

The final stage of the process of returning to this wonderful state of self-awareness is to experience the realisation that the true purpose of love is to be in the service of others. When you know your life's purpose is no more than to serve others, love will have mastered its purpose within you here on earth. The intention of love, is to raise your response rate by bringing about a state of consciousness that will deliver creations of infinite wonder into your world. Actually, you are destined to reach the point where you realise that through your desire to love the world you can consciously change it for the highest good for all concerned.

We hold the power within us to really make a difference. If we develop an attitude of providing service rather than that of exploitation for our own good, the power of love will allow blessings, healing, and miracles to enter every part of your life.

Life is a gift to be shared not spared. I waited a long time for the gift of life to show itself to me and then one day I realised I was that gift. After realising this, the best present I could give anyone was myself. The power is within you to make a difference in the time that you are here. What a difference we will make if we are united in our convictions of this one principle rule of love.

Remember, by application, your love will always grow.

We have looked at how to act upon the forgotten self and apply spiritual practices. I gave you these to use as daily tools in your life. Living and applying all we have learned in the present moment, right now – today, will help every aspect of your life going forward from this point. Your relationship with others, your health, your lifestyle and an understanding of what your true self really is about will grow exponentially as you start to apply what we have talked about. Finally, when you accept love for what it is you will enter a state of deep happiness, understanding first all the barriers that may have appeared in your way.

This story is of your life. There should never be a time that you cannot be yourself. It may appear that your life is all about your situation, your circumstances, the events that are happening or not happening around you, but they are mere paradigms, intellectual perceptions or views. The truth is that whatever is happening in your life can be controlled from within *yourself*.

> ***What you think... you become***
>
> ***What you feel... you attract***
>
> ***What you act on... you create.***

You are the author of your life. Love is quite simply a journey – the journey we all must make if we are to reach our truly deserved destination. Our lives are very short in distance and it would be a great shame to miss out on the experience of how wonderful life itself should be. So, do it now, the divine is waiting.

I would like to invite you to partake of the last spiritual practice that will reconnect you with your higher self and with everyone else around you:

Bless everything you see with love.

Silently, wish love upon everyone you meet; wish them what you would love them to experience. Imagine them to be happy, abundant with life's true riches.

Send blessings to people you might still feel tempted to withhold your love from.

Bless the person you know you have judged the most.

Bless your opponents so you will have no real opposition.

Bless the world everyday with peace.

Bless the animals and all of nature.

Each time we bless the world with love we connect ourselves to a greater power that is within ourselves to make a difference. There is enough love within you to love everything on this planet a million-fold. Begin your own story of love and perhaps tales of the unexpected; tales that can be passed down from generation to generation.

There is a difference between knowing the path of life and actually walking it. Now, it is up to you to take those steps and move your life in the right direction, and when you do it with love, then love will always find you.

I can't predict in detail what love will personally do for you. As I have said, everyone is different, but I do know that one thing is always there for all of us, and that is the invitation. It is laid out in front of you with a clear pathway ahead for the return to love.

Love, Mario.

About The Author

Mario Noviello lives in England, with very strong Italian roots,
his parents being Italian migrants.

He dedicates his time to helping people realise their true spiritual potential, personally sharing his work to spread the message that a true return to love is the way to finding inner peace and joy in abundance.

Printed in Great Britain
by Amazon